PERSONALITY AND DEVELOPMENT IN CHILDHOOD: A PERSON-CENTERED APPROACH

Daniel Hart
Robert Atkins
Suzanne Fegley

WITH COMMENTARY BY
Richard W. Robins and Jessica L. Tracy

Willis F. Overton
Series Editor

MONOGRAPHS OF THE SOCIETY FOR RESEARCH IN CHILD DEVELOPMENT

Serial No. 272, Vol. 68, No. 1, 2003

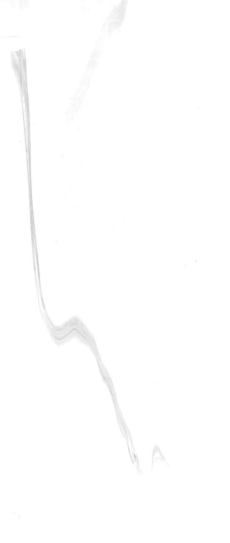

 **Blackwell Publishing**   *Boston, Massachusetts   Oxford, United Kingdom*

EDITOR
WILLIS F. OVERTON
Temple University

EDITORIAL ASSISTANT
MARGARET BERRY
Temple University

CONSULTING EDITORS FOR THE MONOGRAPHS (2003)

PERSONALITY AND DEVELOPMENT IN CHILDHOOD: A PERSON-CENTERED APPROACH

CONTENTS

COMMENTARY

ABSTRACT

HART, DANIEL; ATKINS, ROBERT; FEGLEY, SUZANNE. Personality and Development in Childhood: A Person-Centered Approach. *Monographs of the Society for Research in Child Development*, 2003, **68** (1, Serial No. 272).

A person-centered approach to personality focusing on types of persons defined by profiles of traits is applied to childhood personality development. In 28 diverse samples of 3-, 4-, 5-, and 6-year-olds, three personality types, labeled resilient, overcontrolled, and undercontrolled, are identified. In two longitudinal samples, the undercontrolled type was related to intellectual decline over a period of six years. Both stability and change in childhood personality type were observed in longitudinal analyses. The number of risks characterizing a child's family predicted change in personality type over a two-year interval. Finally, personality type was found to be a moderator of the association of Head Start participation with cognitive development and behavior problems in childhood. The implications of personality type for understanding childhood development, particularly in children facing adversity, are considered.

I. INTRODUCTION

In this *Monograph* we argue that personality—specifically *personality type*, defined as a configuration of personality traits—must be included in a full account of childhood development. The research presented in the *Monograph* is framed within a conceptual framework that focuses on individuals moving through time and context, affecting and receiving influence from their environments. Based on five studies using a diverse, national sample of children, we reach four conclusions. (a) Replicable personality types can be identified in children. (b) These personality types are reliably associated with childhood growth and decline in academic achievement, and the magnitude of this association is roughly equivalent to that observed between academic achievement and family income or home environment. (c) Changes in childhood personality type are correlated in predictable ways with variations in family circumstances. (d) Personality types moderate the association of Head Start (a national early childhood intervention) participation to cognitive and behavioral outcomes.

A PERSON-CENTERED APPROACH TO DEVELOPMENT

The person-centered approach to development that organizes the research presented in this *Monograph* takes as its focus the lives of individuals followed over time. As detailed in the following sections, children are characterized in terms of personality trait profiles as a way of understanding how types of children fare over time academically, to relate changes in a child's personality profile to family circumstances, and, finally, to assess whether a child's profile of personality traits moderates the link between Head Start participation and developmental outcome. For each of these goals, the lens of research is on individual children as they move through time.

1

In this *Monograph*, "person-centered" refers to an approach that uses the individual as the focal unit of analysis. Fundamental to the person-centered approach to research is the postulate that personality is an intrapersonal, dynamic, organized system of psychological processes influencing behavior (e.g., Allport, 1937; Block, 2002). A wide range of personality and developmental theorists have, historically, accepted this postulate (see, e.g., Freud, 1923/1962; Kohlberg, 1984; Loevinger, 1976). Indeed, the notion that personality is organized in some fashion within individuals is so intuitively compelling that (to the best of our knowledge) no personality theorist has ever rejected this postulate.

However, personality *research* during the past century was dominated by investigations that did not examine or reflect the universally accepted postulate of personality organization within individuals. Personality researchers devoted their energies to identifying personality *traits*, which can be defined as dimensions along which are arrayed "individual differences in the tendency to behave, think, and feel in certain consistent ways" (Caspi, 1998, p. 312). The prototypical study of personality measures the correlation of a single personality trait with behaviors that are presumed either to result from or to shape the trait under study. Because the focus is on a personality variable, this line of research can be labeled *variable-centered*.

There are two shortcomings of the traditional variable-centered approach. The first is that the presentation of relations among variables —tables of correlations among variables, path diagrams representing relations in a set of variables—focuses attention on psychological processes *abstracted* from the individuals within whom the processes operate (Runyan, 1984). The presentation of relations among variables also promotes what Lewin (1935) called the myth of the "average child" (p. 68), the belief that children are alike on all dimensions except those that are under study. These are both fictions: Personality processes occur within individuals, and individuals differ in important ways from each other.

The second shortcoming of the variable-centered approach to the study of personality is that the organization of traits within individuals is typically ignored. As Allport (1937) noted, trait research implicitly assumes that personality is "simply the sum-total of the independent factors, thereby committing the fallacy of the omnibus (bundle) conception of personality" (p. 347). Allport argued that a full account of personality must recognize that traits are interconnected and hierarchically organized. The person-centered approach to research seeks to avoid the shortcomings of the trait approach by highlighting persons and the organization of traits within persons.

Methods of Person-Centered Research

Much of the person-centered research in developmental psychology has examined how persons of particular types, characterized by specific organizations of characteristics, move through the life course (Caspi, 1987; Magnusson & Bergman, 1990; Runyan, 1978; Singer, Ryff, Carr, & Magee, 1998; Zhao, Brooks-Gunn, McLanahan, & Singer, 2000). These studies, like all others in the person-centered tradition, are characterized by the *data* judged important to distinguish types and the *analytic techniques* used to identify the types.

What data should be used to identify types? Because theorists posit that personality permeates an individual's thoughts, emotions, and actions, it would be ideal to characterize personality and its organization through an examination of a person's entire life. Biographies come closest to elaborating the intertwining of person and context. The biographical approach is ordinarily reserved for historians, but Singer and colleagues developed a variant that they have applied in the study of large samples of children and adults followed longitudinally (Singer et al., 1998; Zhao et al., 2000). The essence of this approach is that the records—containing thousands of data points—for a small number of participants who represent ideal types are inspected, and biographies for these individuals are written. These biographies are, in turn, analyzed for key variables that distinguish among the ideal types, with these key variables then used in analyses of the larger sample. The advantage of this approach is that it integrates information from many domains of a person's life; a resilient adolescent, for example, can be characterized in terms of relationships, personality, academic achievement, and connections to neighborhood institutions (Singer et al., 1998). However, the findings from this kind of analysis are difficult to replicate in their details because the construction of the initial biographies reflects a multitude of subjective decisions by the investigators. Therefore, this approach may be most useful in the generation of hypotheses. Moreover, by integrating all kinds of data into the account, this form of person-centered research does not lend itself well to the study of the interactions of personality with the environment, a topic of considerable interest to personality researchers.

Types of persons have been more often identified using sources of data specifically relevant to investigators' theoretical goals. For example, Magnusson and Bergman (1990), who were interested in understanding the development of adult maladjustment, grouped adolescent boys according to their profiles of adjustment problems and found that the eight types followed distinct trajectories into adulthood. Runyan (1984) used a person-centered approach to understand occupational development, and characterized men followed longitudinally by their location in the social structure (e.g., from a high-status family, in a high status job), focusing particularly on the likelihood of transition from one location to another. Personality researchers have used personality data to characterize groups of persons (e.g., York & John, 1992), a type of data particularly relevant to this *Monograph*'s focus.

Analytic techniques. Most usually, person-centered research proceeds with the identification of types of persons. The identification of groups of persons is frequently done through cluster analysis (e.g., Magnusson & Bergman, 1990) or Q-factor analysis (e.g., York & John, 1992). The goal of these analytic techniques is to maximize similarity among members of a group while minimizing resemblance of members of one group to members of all the others. Neither analytic technique can be applied mechanically for the identification of types as persons because the determination of the number of groups of persons to be formed is not a precise empirical discovery but instead reflects the judgment and theoretical orientation of the investigators. Moreover, the number of groups that is specified has implications for statistical analysis: If many groups are specified, then there may be few participants in each group, which makes parametric data analysis difficult. On the other hand, the formation of only a few groups may mean that participants have only limited resemblance to other participants in the same group, and consequently viewing this group as representing a type of person can be misleading. There is no easy resolution of this problem, which has led to calls for the development of new analytic techniques for person-centered research (Singer & Ryff, 2001). Of course, the problem is not unique to person-centered research, as the numbers of distinct personality traits or different factors of intelligence are also hotly debated by theorists.

A research example. Cairns, Cairns, and Neckerman's (1989) investigation of the precursors to dropping out of school is an excellent example of the person-centered approach. Personality and academic achievement assessments were made of a sample of young adolescents. The adolescents were then followed longitudinally, allowing the identification of those who dropped out of school. In a preliminary variable-centered analysis, the authors found that aggressive behavior in early adolescence was a predictor of dropping out of school. The variable-centered analysis was augmented with a person-centered analysis. Cluster analysis was used to partition a sample of young adolescent students into seven groups, each of which was defined by a distinctive profile of traits and characteristics. Three of the seven groups are particularly relevant

4

for illustrating the value of the person-centered approach: the aggressive, academically successful group; the nonaggressive, academically failing group; and the aggressive, academically failing group. Adolescents who were assigned to the group characterized by *both* aggression and poor academic performance were at extremely high (82%) risk of dropping out of school prior to graduation. The investigators concluded, "As important as aggressive behavior is in predicting school dropout, its key role is derived in configuration with other problems of adaptation" (Cairns & Cairns, 1994, p. 184). The use of cluster analysis, the emphasis on the organization of traits within the individual, and a presentation of results that highlights the outcomes for individuals rather than relations within a system of variables, all make this investigation representative of the person-centered approach.

Level of Analysis

Because personality is the enduring, organized, dynamic system (e.g., Allport, 1937) that influences thoughts, emotions, and behaviors, personality research must provide answers to questions concerning the *individuals* who generate the thoughts, experience the emotions, and emit the behaviors. Indeed, it is difficult to imagine that a theory of personality could be judged successful if it yielded no interpretative vantage for understanding persons. There is a natural fit between personality research and the person-centered approach.

The person-centered approach should be understood within the context of other analytical approaches to development (Overton, 2003). In particular, Overton identified the person-centered approach as one of a triad of interrelated perspectives, with the other two consisting of the biological and cultural perspectives. Investigations within the biological perspective have been particularly popular in the past 20 years, with many studies of intra-individual genetic and biological processes. Many of these investigations accord explanatory primacy to biological mechanisms that exist and function within all individuals and ignore the connections of these mechanisms to processes occurring at the level of the individual and the culture. However, combining levels of analysis can yield new insights. For example, Kagan, Snidman, McManis, Woodward, and Hardway (2002) suggested that a consideration of the biological mechanisms involved in physiological reactivity can contribute to the clarification of personality typologies. Similarly, Gottlieb and colleagues (Gottlieb, 2002; Gottlieb & Halpern, 2002) illustrated how the understanding of the operation of genetic and biological processes—those involved in the evolution of adaptations—can be enriched by attending to the behaviors that result from the interactions of an organism with its environment. For example,

Gottlieb (2002) suggested that new classes of behaviors enacted by individuals, developed in reaction to new conditions in the environment, can lead to the constellation of conditions for genetic change.

The cultural approach—the third member of the research triad—aims to identify the intertwining of threads of culture and psychological functioning. As Levine (2001) noted, some cultural researchers have assumed that personality and personality differences between individuals are byproducts of the operation of culture and consequently are of little theoretical interest. More informative, however, are investigations that examine the interactions between cultures and personality. For example, recent research suggests that the relation of personality to life satisfaction varies from society to society as a function of the cultural emphasis on individualism (Schimmack, Radhakrishnan, Oishi, Dzokoto, & Ahadi, 2002). Studies have also demonstrated that cultural changes within societies affect the relation of personality to behavior (e.g., Elder, 1998).

The three approaches and the corresponding levels of analysis associated with each are necessary for a full understanding of the complexity of human development. The person-centered approach that organizes the work in this *Monograph* is not intrinsically superior to biological or cultural approaches for understanding development. Indeed, as we shall discuss in chapter VII, many of the questions that arise from the patterns of findings reported in the studies presented here can only be answered from these other two perspectives.

Communication of Findings

The person-centered approach is an appropriate level of analysis for research intended for those making social policy. We believe that our findings in this *Monograph* concerning the association of change in personality type with family risk status, and the association of type with academic trajectory, have implications for early interventions. McCartney and Rosenthal (2000) pointed out that policymakers cannot grasp the magnitude of effects as they are reported in many research reports; consequently McCartney and Rosenthal have called for the use of statistical techniques that highlight practical implications. Rosenthal and Rubin (1982) suggested that the practical importance of correlations between variables could be illustrated by recasting the associations in terms of success rates for individuals (e.g., the death rate for those who do and do not receive an experimental treatment). Person-centered research, because its findings are already presented in terms of types of individuals, offers—at least in part—the advantages for interpretation that are found in Rosenthal and Rubin's procedure.

PERSONALITY TYPE

In this *Monograph*, we apply the person-centered approach to child-hood personality through the identification of *personality types*, characterizing children in terms of types and investigating the relations of these types to important contexts in children's lives. Personality types are configurations of personality traits that distinguish individuals from each other. Conceptually, the typological approach emphasizes persons; groups of children, each group defined by a particular constellation of traits and representing a particular kind of person, are followed through time. The emphasis on functioning individuals rather than on individual traits is one of the potential strengths of personality research (Funder, 2001) and it is particularly salient in the typological approach. In the following sections, we discuss the theoretical and empirical work on personality types.

Theory and Personality Type

Allport and Odbert (1936) estimated that the English language contains 18,000 words that can be used to "distinguish the behavior of one human being from that of another" (Allport, 1937, p. 305). The richness of the language allows infinitely diverse, detailed descriptions of personalities. If each word corresponded to an independent personality disposition, then to generate a profile of an individual's traits would require 18,000 judgments. Moreover, if there were 18,000 traits, all of which were independent of each other and equally important, the ways in which personalities differed from each other would be nearly endless and person-centered personality research would be impossible.

There are good conceptual, empirical, and theoretical reasons to conclude that there are not 18,000 independent, equally important personality traits. First, as Allport and Odbert (1936) noted, there are many synonyms and antonyms among the 18,000 words on their list of personality descriptions. For example, the meaning of "outgoing" is similar to that of "extraverted," and both imply the opposite of "reserved." The 18,000 words can be grouped into classes that share meaning, and this classification results in a much smaller conceptual vocabulary for the characterization of personality. This conceptual analysis has been followed by several decades of factor analytic research that has attempted to identify broad, superordinate dimensions that infuse meaning into the vocabulary used to describe personality. Saucier and Goldberg (2001) reviewed research indicating that much of the meaning in the corpus of trait words can be represented in seven or fewer dimensions. They noted that a five-dimensional characterization is most popular among researchers in the United States, but that across cultures a three-dimensional characterization seems to replicate best. Important for our argument here is that there is considerable consensus that the vast lexicon of personality adjectives can be distilled to a small number of essential dimensions of personality.

Fundamental to the concept of personality types is the recognition that the essential dimensions of personality are *not* functionally independent. As Asendorpf, Borkenau, Ostendorf, & van Aken (2001) pointed out:

> Deriving an efficient set of trait dimensions, and representing personality structure as a point in the multivariate trait space, is not sufficient for the description of personality. It is not sufficient because we do not know how the individual personality patterns are distributed in the multivariate trait space. (p. 170)

In other words, although personality might be described with relatively independent dimensions derived from the factor analysis of trait words, all possible combinations of those dimensions may not occur in real persons. For example, it is theoretically possible for a person to be both high on a trait dimension corresponding to the propensity to experience negative emotions (frequently labeled *neuroticism*) and high on a trait dimension representing achievement motivation (*conscientiousness*), but such a combination is rarely observed (Asendorpf et al., 2001). This is one reason that personality types, which are intended specifically to represent the correlation and organization among traits that occurs within individuals, have been developed.

Personality theory aims to account for the associations among different kinds of traits, and consequently theory guides to some extent the number of personality types that are identified. Jung (1923) proposed a very elaborate theoretical typology for personality, which inspired the development of the Myers-Briggs Type Indicator (MBTI), a personality inventory that permits the identification of 16 personality types. The crucial problem with the MBTI is that the 16 personality types proposed by Jungian theory cannot be identified empirically. For example, Lorr (1991), using cluster-analysis of scale scores from the MBTI to identify types of persons empirically, was able to identify only four replicable personality types, and only two of those corresponded to the 16 types proposed by the theory.

Block's (1977, 2002) model of the basic processes of personality and their role in adaptation has been the most influential theory in the recent renaissance in personality type research. According to Block and Block, personality can be characterized in terms of two broad processes, *ego-control* and *ego-resiliency*. Ego-control refers to the "degree of impulse control and modulation" (J. H. Block & J. Block, 1980, p. 41) characterizing the individual, and ego-resiliency is indicated by the "ability to modify one's behavior in accordance with contextual demands" (p. 48). An individual who is high in ego-resiliency is flexible in impulse control, expressing emotions and impulses when appropriate but containing them when it is necessary to do so. Persons low in ego-resiliency lack this flexibility; those who tend toward impulse expression may become consistent *under-controllers*, and those whose characteristic style is to bind impulse expression may develop into *overcontrollers*. The combination of ego-control and ego-resiliency therefore leads theoretically to three groups: those high in ego-resiliency (and who are flexible in ego-control), those low in ego-resiliency and low in ego-control, and those low in ego-resiliency and high in ego-control.

One attractive feature of the types suggested by Block and Block's theoretical model is that they correspond to the kinds of groups found in studies of childhood psychopathology. Epidemiological studies of childhood adjustment problems (e.g., Achenbach, Howell, Quay, & Conners, 1991) typically find a large group of children with no serious adjustment problems (who would likely be high in ego-resiliency); a group prone to depression, anxiety, and other internalizing symptoms (overcontrollers); and a group characterized by externalizing symptoms such as aggression, delinquent behavior, and substance abuse (undercontrollers). A typology consisting of a well-adjusted type, an overcontrolled type, and an undercontrolled type is therefore consistent with theory and research in childhood psychopathology. In the next section, we review the empirical work on personality types, focusing particularly on childhood.

Research on Personality Types in Childhood

Robins, John, Caspi, Moffitt, and Stouthamer-Loeber (1996) spawned much of the recent interest in childhood personality types. Robins and colleagues used the personality judgments mothers made of their preadolescents to identify personality types. Maternal personality judgments were recorded with the California Child Q-Set (J. Block & J. H. Block, 1980), which consists of 100 personality descriptors. Robins and colleagues split their sample into two subsamples, then used inverse factor analysis (also called *Q-factor analysis*; we discuss this technique in chapter II) in each subsample to identify types of children. Robins et al. found that a three-factor solution, suggestive of three personality types, replicated best across the two samples. They labeled the types *resilient, overcontrolled, and undercontrolled*. The resilient type is characterized by self-confidence, independence, verbal fluency, and an ability to concentrate on tasks; the overcontrolled type is characterized by shyness, quietness, anxiety, and dependability; and the undercontrolled type is characterized by impulsivity, stubbornness, and physical activity. These empirically derived types bore predictable relationships to measures of psychopathology. Boys in the resilient group had the lowest level of problem behaviors (as judged by

9

teachers); overcontrolled boys were most likely to be high in internalizing symptoms, and undercontrolled boys had the highest rates of problem behavior in school and reported the most delinquent behaviors.

Caspi and Silva (1995) used cluster analysis of personality/temperament ratings made by researchers of a large sample of children to identify five personality types in 3-year-olds. The sample was divided into thirds, with cluster analysis of the ratings conducted for each subsample. A five-cluster solution was found to replicate best across the three samples. The authors labeled the five groups to represent their configuration of personality/ temperament characteristics: under-controlled, inhibited, confident, re- served, and well-adjusted. Three of the groups are similar to those identified by Robins et al. (1996). Caspi and Silva's undercontrolled group is characterized by a lack of control, distractibility, and emotional lability; their inhibited group is described by social withdrawal and inhibition in novel situations; finally, their well-adjusted group is characterized as being adaptable to change. These three types—undercontrolled, inhibited, and well-adjusted—correspond to the undercontrolled, overcontrolled, and resilient groups identified by Robins et al. Particularly important for understanding the life course is that Caspi and Silva found that personality type at age 3 is associated with self-reported personality at age 19. For example, children who were included in the inhibited group at age 3 were more likely to score high on a self-report measure of harm avoidance at age 19 than were those who as 3-year-olds were assigned to any of the other groups.

Since publication of Robins et al. (1996) and Caspi and Silva (1995), a handful of other studies have identified personality types in childhood and adolescence, including Asendorpf and van Aken (1999), Dubas, Gerris, Janssens, and Vermulst (2002), Hart, Hofmann, Edelstein, and Keller (1997), and Weir and Gjerde (2002). We review findings specific to each of these studies in later chapters. Important here are three sets of findings from this body of work. First, there is convergence among these studies on a typology constituted of resilient, overcontrolled, and undercontrolled. Second, the research finds a consistent association of the overcontrolled type with behaviors symptomatic of internalization, and the correlation of the undercontrolled type with externalizing behavior.

Third, the studies by Asendorpf and van Aken (1999), Dubas et al. (2002), Hart et al. (1997), and Weir and Gjerde (2002), demonstrated that personality types are associated with constructs at different explanatory levels in personality theory. As Revelle (1995) and Hair and Graziano (in press) have pointed out, personality traits (and, by implication, personality types) are connected to thought and behavior, but they are also connected to relatively specific, context-dependent psychological processes that exert their own influence on cognition and behavior. These intervening psychological processes include self-evaluation and social strategies (Hair & Graziano) and intelligence, interpersonal skills, and well-being (Revelle). Research findings suggest that childhood personality types are associated with these kinds of psychological processes. Hart et al. (1997) demonstrated that self-evaluation, reasoning about friendship, and patterns of social interaction are associated with personality types; Asendorpf and van Aken (1999) showed that personality types are correlated with intelligence; Weir and Gjerde (2002) found that childhood personality types are associated with adolescent drug use; and Dubas et al. (2002) identified connections between childhood personality types and patterns of emotions. Together, these studies suggest that personality types defined by organizations of personality traits also have predictable relations with psychological constructs that are presumed to have their own connections to behavior.

Research with adults has tended to find personality types similar to those identified in childhood. Block (1971) identified five types of male participants and six types of female participants, based on inverse factor analysis of personality ratings of young adults. Two of these types resemble the resilient and overcontrolled types identified in children. Similarly, York and John (1992) used inverse factor analysis of personality ratings of a sample of middle-aged women to identify four personality types, again finding types that could be labeled resilient and overcontrolled.

More recent research on personality types in adulthood generally has identified a typology very similar to the resilient/overcontrolled/under-controlled typology representing the consensus among childhood research-ers. Asendorpf et al. (2001) presented analyses from three samples of adults and one sample of children that indicated that the typology constituted of resilient, overcontrolled, and undercontrolled groups could be found in all four samples. These researchers, like Caspi (1998), concluded that this typology is replicable across types of data, analytic techniques, age ranges, and Western cultures.

Controversies in the Study of Personality Type

Because personality types reflect organization of traits within indivi-duals, they are extremely useful for this *Monograph*'s person-centered examination of childhood personality. As noted in earlier sections, characterizing personality in terms of independent traits is not an effective strategy for a person-centered account. Our decision to use personality types to characterize childhood personality flows from our goal of presenting a person-centered account of personality, and not from a rejection of personality trait research. Indeed, personality type research is most useful as a complement to, not a competitor with, variable-centered approaches (Horn, 2001). However, there are some theorists and

11

researchers who have placed the personality type and variable-centered approaches in opposition, in order to measure the success of one against the other.

One important theoretical debate has developed in connection with the psychological nature of personality types. Some researchers interpret the empirical evidence to indicate that the threefold typology of resilient/overcontrolled/undercontrolled corresponds to distinguishable classes of individuals, with these groups constituting "fuzzy types" (Asendorpf et al., 2001). Such an interpretation suggests that there are three basic forms of personality functioning—corresponding to the three types—and consequently the internal organization of any single individual ought to be represented by one of the types. The opposing view is that the threefold typology of resilient/overcontrolled/undercontrolled is a convenient summary for the traits from which the types are constituted (e.g., Costa, Herbst, McCrae, Samuels, & Ozer, 2002), but it does not contribute new information to the study of personality. Like York and John (1992) and Robins et al. (1996), we take an intermediate position in this debate. From this intermediate position, personality types correspond to *prototypes* of forms of psychological functioning. Similarity to a personality prototype varies quantitatively; for example, the degree to which an individual resembles the resilient prototype can be assessed, just as the same person's similarity to the undercontrolled prototype can be measured. According to this perspective, labeling someone as belonging to the resilient personality type means that the individual resembles this type more than the other two. The prototype interpretation preserves the notion that types correspond to integrations of traits and processes without the claim that these integrations constitute separate classes of psychological processing.

A second area of debate concerns the relative capability of personality types and personality traits to predict behavior. Some researchers have found that personality types lead to more powerful predictions than do traits. For example, Asendorpf and van Aken (1999) found that childhood personality types are better predictors of later development than are the variables of ego-control and ego-resiliency. Consequently, they concluded that the personality type approach should be preferred over personality variables in longitudinal investigations. Findings from other studies suggest a different conclusion. Costa et al. (2002) reported that continuous personality variable scores are more powerful predictors of a range of measures of psychosocial functioning than are personality types. In chapter IV, we seek to address this controversy by comparing the value of personality types and personality traits to the prediction of academic achievement studied longitudinally.

Both debates—whether types identify classes of individuals or are vague summaries of variables, and whether types or variables allow more

12

powerful predictions—help sharpen the understanding of both types and variables. However, in our view, it is unlikely that either debate will be decisively won by the accretion of new research findings (trait researchers will not abandon their paradigm after reading chapter IV, for example) as personality type research and personality variable research are divided as much by level of analysis and theoretical orientation as they are by empirical phenomena. For this reason we do not try to martial evidence in this *Monograph* to demonstrate the empirical domination of types over variables. Like others (e.g., Asendorpf, 2000), we believe that both person-centered and variable-centered research can contribute to the understanding of personality. In chapters II–VI, we provide evidence that a person-centered, personality type approach can yield valuable insights into the course of development.

PERSONALITY IN CONTEXT

It is a truism of the developmental approach that psychological functioning influences, and is influenced by, the contexts of life. A central goal in this *Monograph* is to explore the relations among personality types and contexts as these occur in the life course of children. Runyan (1984) described three sets of relations, or processes, that need to be explored in life course investigations:

> (1) *Behavior-determining processes*, resulting from the interaction of persons with situations, (2) *person-determining processes*, or the processes that create, maintain, and change personal states and characteristics, and (3) *situation-determining processes*, or the processes through which people select, create, and influence the situations they encounter. (pp. 84–85)

In chapters IV–VI, we use longitudinal research to examine each of these processes; chapter IV reports research relevant to behavior-determining processes, chapter V examines factors associated with change in personality type (person-determining processes), and chapter VI assesses the moderating role of personality type on the relation of Head Start participation to change in problem behavior. We discuss each of these themes below.

Personality Type and the Rate of Academic Achievement

Chapter IV examines the association of personality type to the rate of academic development, a line of investigation that concerns personality type as a behavior-determining process. In the United States and in other industrialized societies, childhood academic achievement has substantial implications for economic success in adulthood. It is for this reason that schools and education more generally have received so much critical attention in the media. We hypothesized that undercontrolled children, characterized by impulsiveness, aggressiveness, and concentration problems, are less likely to engage in behaviors that are conducive to learning than are resilient or overcontrolled children. Confirmation of this hypothesis requires evidence that undercontrolled children *develop at a slower rate* in the academic domain over the course of childhood than children of the other two types. Evidence of an association of childhood personality type and rate of academic development is consistent with the postulate that personality influences the course of life.

To date, the relation of personality to cognition has largely escaped the attention of researchers (for a discussion of the lack of research on this topic, see Endler, 2000). Indeed, some reviews of the research literature conclude that there are no systematic demonstrations of the influence of noncognitive intra-individual factors like personality on academic achievement (e.g., Entwisle, 1990). There are a few lines of work that do indicate that academic achievement is influenced by some noncognitive, intra-individual factors. For example, Hair and Graziano (in press) as well as Marsh and Yeung (1997) have demonstrated that self-evaluations of academic ability are predictors of subsequent academic achievement, even after statistically controlling for concurrent academic achievement. Inattentiveness and disruptiveness in the classroom—patterns of behavior presumably connected to personality—are also associated with poor academic performance (Finn, Pannozzo, & Voelkl, 1995). However, there is a dearth of evidence to indicate that broad personality traits, or personality types, predict to later academic achievement after statistically controlling for concurrently measured academic achievement.

The lack of compelling evidence is probably due in part to the multidetermined nature of academic achievement. When a class or pattern of behaviors—like academic achievement and learning—has multiple determinants, the magnitude of correlation between any one of those determinants and the set of behaviors is far below the theoretical limit of 1. Ahadi and Diener (1989) demonstrated that for very simple systems in which two related behaviors are completely determined by overlapping sets of four predictors, the correlation of any single predictor with any one of the behaviors has an upper bound of approximately .45, not 1.0. The implication of this analysis is that the detection and characterization of the role of personality on academic achievement require investigations with sufficient power to detect small effects, which in turn requires samples much larger than those typical of developmental and educational research. In this *Monograph*, we use a longitudinal design with two large samples to assess the association of personality on the rate of academic development.

Change in Personality as a Function of Environmental Risks

Personality is not immutable; it is influenced by the contexts of development. In chapter V we examine person-changing processes, specifically the correlates of change in personality types. Change in personality is likely to occur slowly. Cairns and Cairns (1994, p. 246) suggested that "constraints from without and from within, and ... the correlated action of external and internal forces" lead development to be "conservative." These constraints and forces may include stable biological tendencies—fearfulness or reactivity, for example—that contribute to personality (e.g., Kagan, 1998), as well as continuities in "parental demands, peer influences, and teacher expectancies" (Caspi, 1998, p. 352) that together serve to stabilize personality. Nonetheless, for personality to serve its theoretical function as the locus of integration for psychological functioning (Funder, 2001), it must be open to change.

Because change is likely to be slow and multidetermined, making identification of factors associated with change more difficult, we strive to maximize the likelihood for detecting person-changing processes by examining the powerful influences of poverty, family structure, and home environment on transformation in personality. These three factors—poverty, family structure, and home environment—are correlated with each other and with indices of childhood success such as academic achievement and problem behaviors (see, e.g., Ackerman, Kogos, Youngstrom, Schoff, & Izard, 1999; Duncan, Brooks-Gunn, Yeung, & Smith, 1998; Korenman, Miller, & Sjaastad, 1995). Further, there is reason to believe that this set of poverty-related factors is likely to be associated with personality development. For example, poverty and a bad home environment are negatively correlated with the development of an adaptive personality (Rutter, 2000). In their review of the literature on the relation of socioeconomic status and child development, Bradley and Corwyn (2002) concluded that family affluence is negatively correlated with externalizing behavior problems. Translated into the terms of personality types, these patterns of findings suggest that for some children the stress of prolonged poverty might undermine the development and maintenance of positive adaptive coping processes, contributing to the degeneration of their resilient personality.

Personality as a Moderator of the Association of Head Start Participation to Developmental Outcomes

Situation-determining processes constitute the third group in Runyan's triumvirate of transactions in the life course. The constellation of traits constituting a personality type influences a child's behaviors, thoughts, and emotions. Children of different types can be expected to behave, think, and feel differently from each other, even when they are in the same environments. In other words, children in the same environment effectively transform it into different environments that reflect their personalities. This axiom of personality theory implies that research should be able to identify *interactions* between personality type and contexts. Specifically, individuals' responses to similar contexts ought to vary according to their personality types.

In this *Monograph*, we examine the interaction of personality type with Head Start participation and family risk status. We believe that the interactions among personality, Head Start participation, and family risk status are fertile grounds for investigation for a number of reasons.

First, Head Start, a national program funded by the U.S. government, ought to have considerable influence on children's lives. It was (and is) a program largely aimed at children whose family circumstances are adverse (United States General Accounting Office, 2002), and consequently the program aims to provide a range of supplemental services (education, nutrition, medical) to its recipients. The range of services offered over an extended period of time (a year or more) is of considerable advantage to children in difficult circumstances, and consequently those receiving these services ought to prosper in comparison to children in comparable circumstances who are not receiving the services.

Second, although there has been surprisingly little research of the long-term effects of Head Start on its participants (United States General Accounting Office, 1997), longitudinal research on participation in preschool interventions serving disadvantaged populations—programs like Head Start—indicates that enrollees benefit as much in terms of social and personality development as they do academically (Crane, 1998). This suggests that the personality system is influenced by Head Start participation.

Third, interactions are suggested by the complexity of findings that emerge from reviews of the long-term effects of Head Start and similar programs on children. Research on some very well-designed interventions for young children have failed to detect main effects for program participation, and for some other interventions the main effects are weak and sometimes perplexing (for a review, see Ferran, 2000). One hypothesis for this pattern of findings is that the effects of program participation vary as a function of personality.

For all these reasons, then, the intersections of personality type with Head Start participation ought to reveal interactions. Moreover, such interactions would have implications for social policy.

SAMPLE

In all five studies, we make use of the *Children of the National Longitudinal Survey of Youth, 1979* (C-NLSY79) data set, which is the product of the

United States Bureau of Labor Statistics (1995). In 1979, the Bureau of Labor Statistics initiated a longitudinal study of young adults (*National Longitudinal Survey of Youth, 1979*; hereafter, NLSY79). The goal was to chart young adults' entry into the labor force, and to assess the influence of education, training, family, and other factors on successful transition into employment (the description of the study found here is based on the report by the Center for Human Resource Research, 1999). The original sample was composed of three groups: a nationally representative sample of 6,111 youth born between January 1, 1957 and December 31, 1964 (ages 14–21 years on 12/31/78; 51% were females); a supplemental sample of 5,295 economically disadvantage youth of the same ages (51% females); and a supplemental sample of 1280 young adults ages 17–21 serving in the military (36% females). Participants were interviewed annually from 1979 until 1994, and biennially from 1994 to 2000, about a range of topics relevant to the labor market. By 1980, most of the participants in the military sample were no longer in military service, and consequently they were dropped from the study. In 1990, the Bureau of Labor Statistics decided to drop White participants from the supplemental sample of economically disadvantaged youth.

The samples for the studies in this *Monograph* are constituted of the children born to the women in the above-described NLSY79. Beginning in 1986, a variety of information about the children of the women in the NLSY was collected biennially. Some of this information was collected through maternal report, some through tests administered by a trained researcher and the same researcher's use of rating scales, and some through self-report (for older children). We describe the measures and data in detail in the following chapters.

In every longitudinal investigation, there is some attrition. This was true for the C-NLSY, although the rate is respectably low. Approximately 90% of participants who were assessed at one measurement point were assessed at the next point; participants who were not assessed at one point were oftentimes successfully recruited back into the study at the subsequent testing point (Mott, 1998). In general, participants who were young, performed well on the measures, and had well-educated mothers were most likely to be retested at subsequent measurement points (Mott, 1998). We discuss attrition effects again in chapters IV–VI, which present longitudinal analyses.

The constitution of the sample for the C-NLSY offers two strengths particularly important for the goals of this project. First, the sample is large. For many analyses reported in the following chapters, there are thousands of participants. With such large samples, small effect sizes can be detected and replication studies can be conducted. Second, the sample is ethnically and economically diverse. Most of the children in the study were born to a representative sample of American women, which ensures that findings are likely to generalize well to other samples. Moreover, the subsample of children born to the women in the economically disadvantaged supplemental sample increases the number of participants available for analyses concerning the relation of factors associated with poverty to personality, a topic of particular interest in this study.

OVERVIEW

Chapters II–VI present four sets of analyses, each accompanied by a brief discussion. Chapters II and III focus on identifying personality types in diverse samples of children and examining cross-sectional associations of personality type with academic achievement and behavior problems. We focused on 6- and 5-year-olds, respectively, in these two chapters, as it is only for children in these age ranges that data for all three areas —personality, academic achievement, and behavior problems—are available. The analyses in chapter IV assess the associations of personality type to rates of academic achievement assessed over time. Chapter V investigates the association of personality change to poverty-related risk factors. Chapter VI examines the interaction of stress, enrollment in Head Start, and personality type in the prediction of academic achievement and behavior problems. Chapter VII provides a general discussion of the findings, an examination of questions that are not answered in the earlier chapters, and some suggestions for future research and policy.

II. PERSONALITY TYPES OF 6-YEAR-OLDS AND THEIR ASSOCIATIONS WITH ACADEMIC ACHIEVEMENT AND BEHAVIOR

Key to the program of research reported in this *Monograph* is the identification of personality types. As we noted in chapter I, previous research has converged on a threefold typology, with profiles labeled resilient, overcontrolled, and undercontrolled. Moreover, these profiles have shown associations with measures of academic achievement and problem behavior. Our goals in this chapter are to (a) determine whether these three personality types can be identified in the data of the NLSY and (b) assess the relationships of the three types to indices of academic achievement and behavior.

IDENTIFICATION OF TYPES

Research on personality types in children has largely relied on inverse factor analysis of ipsative ratings of personality made using the California Child Q-Sort (CCQ; for studies of this type, see Asendorpf & van Aken, 1999; Hart et al., 1997; Robins et al., 1996). *Inverse factor analysis*, or Q-technique factor analysis, is identical mathematically to the more common applications of factor analysis (sometimes labeled *R-technique factor analysis*) for which the goal is to identify latent variables, or factors. The difference between inverse factor analysis and R-technique factor analysis is that the former factors persons and the latter factors variables. R-technique analyses result in the identification of factors, or latent variables, corresponding to related variables. The result of the application of inverse factor analyses is the identification of factors, or prototypes, corresponding to types of persons (Thompson, 2000, provides a useful introduction). For this reason inverse factor analysis has been widely used in research on personality type. We make use of this technique in the studies that follow to identify initial prototypes corresponding to the three personality types described in chapter I.

The CCQ has two noteworthy advantages for the identification of personality types through inverse factor analysis. First, the CCQ was designed to permit the comprehensive characterization of diverse personalities in childhood (J. Block & J. H. Block, 1969/1980). The items in the CCQ cover an unusually broad range of personality features: affective tone, social skills, emotion regulation, and so forth. Consequently, the CCQ provides data on most areas that are central to personality theorizing.

Second, the CCQ yields ipsative data, which are particularly useful for factor analysis. Each of the 100 personality items in the CCQ is sorted into a fixed distribution according to its judged salience in the target individual. This process yields ipsative data, with the distribution of scores for the 100 personality items exactly the same for every participant. Recall that in inverse factor analysis participants are factored. The input for inverse factor analysis is the matrix of correlations among participants. Because the distributions of scores for all participants are exactly the same, correlations among participants are not attenuated by differences in distributions (Thompson, 2000). This ought to permit more accurate identification of factors, or prototypes of persons.

One goal of the study reported in this chapter was to determine whether personality types, similar to those identified in Q-sort data, could be identified in a small number of maternal ratings of childhood personality. Because we used only 20 personality items, and they are nonipsative, the conditions for identification of personality types were less favorable than they are when using Q-sort data. However, there are important and substantial advantages to ratings of a small number of items compared to the complex judgment process necessary for the Q-sort process. In this study, mothers were asked to rate their children on 20 five-point scales. This task was simple, could be done without instruction by a researcher, and was completed in a short period of time. These economies permitted data to be collected for thousands of children, a sample size 10 times larger than any of the samples using Q-sort data to identify childhood personality types. Thus, if personality types can be identified in the small number of maternal ratings found in the NLSY, then the study's vast sample and broad range of variables can be drawn upon in clarifying the relation of personality type to demographic and psychological factors.

Associations of Types With Academic Achievement and Behavior

A second goal in this study was to determine whether personality types identified in maternal ratings resemble those derived from Q-sort data. Two paths were followed. First, we compared the prototypes drawn from the two types of data to determine whether there were conceptual resemblances. Second, we tested whether personality types identified in maternal ratings bore the same relations to cognitive and behavioral ratings as have been found in previous research with Q-sort data. Specifically, we assessed the relationship of personality type to academic achievement. Previous research has demonstrated that children of the undercontrolled type receive lower scores on standardized tests of achievement than do resilient children (Hart et al., 1997; Robins et al., 1996). Replication of this pattern suggests congruence between personality types derived from maternal ratings (this study) and personality types identified in Q-sort data (Hart et al; Robins et al).

Next, we assessed the relation of personality type to behavioral ratings. Robins et al. (1996) found that overcontrolled children are more likely than children of the other two types to have the characteristics of an internalizing disorder, and undercontrolled children are more likely than resilient or overcontrolled children to be characterized as belonging to an externalizing diagnostic group. We sought to replicate this pattern in the analyses that follow.

Finally, personality types derived from maternal ratings of personality were used to predict researchers' ratings of the children in the testing situation. We predicted that researchers would judge (a) the overcontrolled children to be shyer than children of the other two types and (b) the undercontrolled children to be less engaged and cooperative than other children.

METHOD

Participants

Participants were children who were 6 years old at one of the seven testing times (1986, 1988, 1990, 1992, 1994, 1996, 1998) and who had maternal ratings for each of the 20 personality items (described below). What are called personality items here are labeled "temperament" items in the NLSY. Of the 2603 participants (51% male), 22% were Hispanic, 30% were Black, and 48% were White.

Measures

All assessments in this study were conducted when the participants were 6 years old.

Personality. Using a 5-point scale ranging from 0 = almost never to 4 = almost always, mothers judged their children on 20 personality items (the items are presented in Table 1). Although most scales ask for

TABLE 1

TEMPERAMENT ITEMS RANKED IN ORDER OF DESCRIPTIVENESS FOR THE THREE PERSONALITY TYPES

Resilient		Overcontrolled		Undercontrolled	
Temperament Item	Mean	Temperament Item	Mean	Temperament Item	Mean
Obeys and quits TV when told	0.38	Shy with new child	1.09	Gets upset when left alone	.47
Obeys/goes to bed when told	0.36	Shy with new adult	1.04	Is difficult to calm	.42
Quits TV without protest	0.23	Obeys and quits TV when told	.33	Stays close to mom	.41
Obeys and eats when told	0.20	Quits TV without protest	.27	Demanding when mom is busy	.39
Eats what he/she is supposed to eat	0.17	Obeys/goes to bed when told	.23	Often fights with other children	.38
Shares with other children	0.16	Cries when hurt	.21	Wants help	.30
Laughs/smiles easily	0.16	Stays close to mom	.18	Cries when hurt	.18
Sleeps through the night	0.10	Resists going to bed	.08	Copies how mom acts	.13
Gets upset when mom upset	0.04	Copies how mom acts	.08	Resists going to bed	.09
Resists going to bed	−.07	Shares with other children	.06	Shy with new adult	−.13
Copies how mom acts	−.08	Is difficult to calm	.03	Shy with new child	−.14
Often fights with other children	−.08	Obeys and eats when told	.03	Gets upset when mom upset	−.15
Wants help	−.09	Gets upset when left alone	.02	Sleeps through the night	−.21
Demanding when mom is busy	−.14	Gets upset when mom upset	.02	Laughs/smiles easily	−.29
Cries when hurt	−.18	Eats what he/she is supposed to eat	.01	Eats what he/she is supposed to eat	−.42
Is difficult to calm	−.18	Wants help	−.02	Obeys and eats when told	−.50
Gets upset when left alone	−.21	Sleeps through the night	−.03	Shares with other children	−.51
Stays close to mom	−.27	Demanding when mom is busy	−.03	Quits TV without protest	−.96
Shy with new adult	−.55	Laughs/smiles easily	−.04	Obeys/goes to bed when told	−1.19
Shy with new child	−.58	Often fights with other children	−.09	Obeys and quits TV when told	−1.43

typicality (e.g., "how characteristic ...") rather than the frequency judgments required by this measure, both kinds of judgments yield information on the descriptiveness of an item for an individual.

Achievement. A trained researcher administered to each child three subtests (mathematics, reading recognition, reading comprehension) from the Peabody Individual Achievement Test (PIAT). Scores on each subtest were standardized to have a mean of 100 and a standard deviation of 15 (standard scores were based on a 1969 norming sample for the Peabody). The average of the scores on the three subtests was used as the summary index of academic achievement (alpha for this composite of scores = .79).

Behavior problems. Mothers recorded judgments of their children on the Behavior Problems Index (BPI), for which there is a total score (alpha = .88 in the NLSY; see Baker, Keck, Mott, & Quinlan, 1993) and subscales for six types of problems. These subscales (and their reliabilities as reported in the NLSY Handbook; see Baker et al.) are Antisocial behavior (alpha = .67), Anxiousness/Depression (alpha = .65), Headstrongness (alpha = .71), Hyperactivity (alpha = .69), Immaturity/Dependency (alpha = .62), and Peer conflict/Social withdrawal (alpha = .57). In the following analyses, we used the standard scores (based on a national norming sample, the average for each subtest set at 100 and a standard deviation of 15; sample means and standard deviations are presented in Table 2) for these six problem types.

Behavior ratings. At the completion of the administration of the PIAT test to the child, the researcher rated the child on six behavior items: (a) shyness/anxiety at the beginning of the session, (b) shyness/anxiety at the end of the session, (c) rapport with the researcher, (d) perseverance/persistence in the tests, (e) cooperation, and (f) motivation/interest. The two shyness ratings were made using a scale ranging from 1 = not at all shy or anxious/sociable and friendly to 5 = extremely shy/quite/withdrawn. The scales for the other four ratings also ranged from 1 to 5, and were anchored at the extremes with the labels "Poor" and "Excellent."

RESULTS

Derivation of Types

A random number generator was used to assign to each participant a number between 1 and 7. The generator produced roughly equal numbers

TABLE 2

MULTIPLE REGRESSION RESULTS FOR EQUATIONS PREDICTING BEHAVIOR PROBLEM TOTAL SCORE AND SUBSCALE SCORES

Behavior Problem	Resilient (0)/ Overcontrolled (1) Contrast			Resilient (0)/ Undercontrolled (1) Contrast			R for Equation	M for Sample	SD for Sample
	B	SEB	Beta	B	SEB	Beta			
Total score	.77	.76	.02	7.49	.87	.21*	.20	105.01	14.56
Anxiety/Depression	2.83	.65	.10*	6.06	.76	.19*	.18	102.37	12.92
Dependency	2.15	.67	.07*	6.83	.77	.20*	.19	104.31	13.27
Peer withdrawal/Conflict	2.30	.68	.08*	4.70	.78	.14*	.14	105.22	13.20
Antisocial	−.68	.70	−.02	5.46	.80	.16*	.17	105.34	13.38
Headstrong	−.72	.67	−.03	4.40	.76	.14*	.15	100.56	12.93
Hyperactive	−1.40	.72	−.04	4.34	.83	.12*	.14	105.61	14.04

Note.—There were 1894 to 1987 participants for each of the reported equations.
*$p < .05$.

of each digit. These numbers were then used to divide the full sample into seven subsamples, ranging in size from 345 to 411 participants.

For each subsample, an inverse factor analysis was conducted on the personality ratings. The matrix of participants by personality ratings for each subsample was transposed, and then submitted to principal components analysis. To maintain comparability with previous research, a varimax rotation and three-component (factor) solution were specified for each analysis. The product of each analysis was three factors, with each factor representing a personality prototype defined by the personality items.

To determine the extent of convergence in factor solutions across the seven random samples, factor scores (regression method) for each of the 20 personality items, for each factor, in each of the 7 principal components solutions, were computed. The vector of factor scores for the first factor in one solution was then correlated with the vector of factor scores for all other factors in each of the other solutions; the same procedure was followed with the vectors of scores for the second and third factors. These correlations are presented in Appendix A. The convergence correlations are those for the same factor from different samples. Almost all convergence correlations were greater than .80, indicating substantial convergence in factors across the seven subsamples.

Because the matrix of participants by personality ratings was transposed prior to principal components analysis, each participant received a factor loading on each of the three factors, with each factor representing a prototype. These factor loadings were used to assign participants to preliminary personality prototypes, following the procedure described by Robins et al. (1996, p. 161) in which participants were assigned to preliminary prototypes if (a) their factor loading was equal to or greater than .4, (b) their second highest factor loading score was .2 less than the highest score, and (c) at least one factor loading score was less than .4. Following these procedures, 1500 (58%) participants could be assigned to a preliminary prototype.

These preliminary prototypes were used to identify centers for the cluster analysis that was used in the final step of assignment of participants to personality types (for a similar two-step procedure, see Caspi & Silva, 1995). The starting points for the cluster analysis were determined by calculating average scores for the 20 standardized personality ratings for all participants assigned to each preliminary prototype. The means for the 20 standardized personality ratings for each preliminary prototype were used as starting points for a k-means cluster analysis (SPSS quick cluster routine, with a three-cluster solution specified). The cluster analysis procedure resulted in the assignment of each participant to one cluster, or personality prototype.

25

Table 1 presents the 20 personality items, rank-ordered according to descriptiveness (mean standardized score for the type) for each of the three final personality types. Personality items suggestive of compliant, cooperative behavior, positive emotion, and a lack of shyness characterized the *resilient* type. Clear parallels to the resilient personality types in previous research can be identified. For example, Hart et al. (1997) found the traits "obedient and compliant" to be particularly characteristic of resilient children and Robins et al. (1996) found the traits "likes to laugh" and a "lack of shyness" to be most characteristic of the resilient type in their study.

In this study, children of the overcontrolled type were rated as shy, compliant, and dependent. Again, these characteristics are similar to those defining the overcontrolled type in previous research. In both the Hart et al. (1997) and Robins et al. (1996) studies, shyness was one of the most characteristic traits of the overcontrolled type, and Hart et al. found dependency ("looks to adults for help") to be descriptive as well.

Finally, from Table 1 it is apparent that undercontrolled children have difficulty regulating emotion, are dependent, aggressive, resistant to adult authority, and disagreeable. Robins et al. (1996), as well as Asendorpf and van Aken (1999), reported that the unregulated expression of emotion and a lack of obedience are characteristic of the undercontrolled type.

Distribution of Types

As noted previously, the sample was made up of *all* children born to a nearly representative sample of American women; therefore some participants had siblings in the study. The resulting interdependencies among data points violates the assumptions of most statistical significance tests, so to avoid this problem we used only one child from each family (the oldest eligible participant, following the precedent of Emery, Waldron, Kitzmann, & Aaron, 1999) in the remaining analyses reported in this chapter. As a result, the number of participants was reduced by approximately 25%, from the 2603 used for the derivation of types to 1991. Furthermore, because of missing data, the number of participants available for some analyses was less than 1991.

In this study, 1010 (50%) of the children were assigned to the resilient type (47% girls), 586 (29%) to the overcontrolled type (34% girls), and 395 (20%) to the undercontrolled type (17% girls). The association between type and gender was weak but statistically reliable ($\chi^2 = 19.71$, $p < .05$). The distributions of types, and their association with gender, resembled the findings of Asendorpf and van Aken (1999), who found that 49% of the children in their sample were assigned to the resilient type, and that boys were more likely than girls to be categorized as undercontrolled.

Functional Similarities to Personality Types Identified in Previous Research

In previous research, the three personality types were found to predict academic achievement/intellectual ability and internalizing/externalizing syndromes (Asendorpf & van Aken, 1999; Hart et al. 1997; Robins et al. 1996).

Achievement. Asendorpf and van Aken (1999) and Robins et al. (1996) found that undercontrolled children receive lower scores than do children of the other two types, who do not differ from each other. The mean scores for the three Peabody achievement tests for the three types reflect this pattern: 102.6, 101.9, and 99.1 for the resilient, overcontrolled, and undercontrolled types, respectively (for the sample, $M = 101.9$, $SD = 9.9$). We assessed the reliability of differences among these means using multiple regression with dummy codes to represent the three personality types (dummy code for overcontrolled is coded 1 for children of the overcontrolled type and 0 for the other two; dummy code for undercontrolled is coded 1 for children of the undercontrolled type and 0 for children of the other two types). Only the dummy variable for the undercontrolled contrast was significant (undercontrolled contrast: $B = -3.46$, $SE = .60$, $\beta = -.14$, $p < .01$; overcontrolled contrast: $B = -.71$, $SE = .52$, $\beta = -.03$; $R = .13$, $N = 1886$).

Behavior problems. Robins et al. (1996) found that children rated as undercontrolled were more likely than other children to be classified in an externalizing diagnostic group and that children of the overcontrolled type, in comparison to other children, had a heightened probability of belonging to the internalizing diagnostic group. Robins and his colleagues formed diagnostic groups by using the 80th percentiles as cutoff scores on scales of internalizing and externalizing behavior. Children above the 80th percentile on both measures were assigned to a multiproblem group, children above the 80th percentile on the internalizing scale but below the 80th percentile on the externalizing scale were assigned to the internalizing group, children above the 80th percentile on the externalizing scale and below the 80th percentile on the internalizing scale were considered to belong to the externalizing group, and children below the 80th percentile on both scales were assigned to the psychopathology-free group. The association between personality type and diagnostic group was then tested.

We used scores on the Depression/Anxiety and the Antisocial scales of the BPI as measures of internalizing and externalizing behavior, respectively. Each scale has a mean of 100 and a standard deviation of 15 in the national norming sample. We used these scales to form

27

diagnostic groups following a procedure similar to that outlined by Robins et al. (1996). Participants with internalizing (Depression/Anxiety) scores above 112 (approximately the 80th percentile in the norming sample) and externalizing (Antisocial) scores below 112 were assigned to the internalizing group. Those with externalizing scores greater than or equal to 112 and those with scores less than 112 on the internalizing measure were assigned to the externalizing group. Participants with scores equal to or greater than 112 on both scales were assigned to the multiproblem group, and those with scores lower than 112 on both scales were categorized in the no-problem group.

Figure 1 presents the percentage of participants in each personality type belonging to each diagnostic group. The association of personality type to diagnostic group was significant (χ^2 [1888] = 67.42, $p < 01$). Consistent with the Robins et al. (1996) research, undercontrolled children were assigned to the externalizing group more often than children of the other two types (31% of undercontrolled children were in this diagnostic group, compared to 27% and 25% of the resilient and overcontrolled children, respectively). Similarly, 10% of overcontrolled

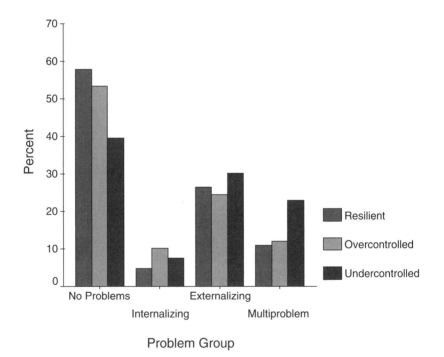

FIGURE 1.—Percentage of 6-year-old participants of each personality type in each problem group.

children, but only 5% of the resilient and 7% of the undercontrolled children, were assigned to the internalizing group. Although the pattern of relations of personality type to diagnostic group is consistent with expectations, the association of type and diagnostic group is fairly weak. For example, 26% of children assigned to the resilient type are characterized by their mothers in such a way that they are assigned to the externalizing problem group.

The incomplete overlap of type and diagnostic group is further suggested by the fact that overcontrolled children are more likely to be assigned to the externalizing problem group than they are to the internalizing group. However, this apparently anomalous finding is largely explained by the fact that there were four times as many participants in the externalizing group than in the internalizing group, and as a consequence the baseline probability for assignment to the externalizing group was quite high for all participants. The difference in baseline probabilities for assignment to the two groups suggests that the behavior problem items probably are better at tapping externalizing behavior than internalizing behavior. A principal components analysis of the six subscale scores yielded only one factor with an eigenvalue greater than 1, indicating that mothers' ratings of their children's problem behaviors on this scale were not well-differentiated (this problem has been noted by other investigators using the NLSY; see, e.g., Emery et al., 1999).

Figure 1 also suggests that in comparison to resilient and overcontrolled children, undercontrolled children were generally perceived by their mothers as having more problems. The trend for mothers of undercontrolled children to judge that their children have more behavior problems than mothers of children of the other two types is particularly evident when the six behavior problem subscales are considered individually, rather than jointly to define groups as in the previous analysis. Figure 2 depicts the average scores for total behavior problems and each of the six problem subscales for the three personality types. As is evident in Figure 2, undercontrolled children had the highest average scores for total problems and for all six problem subscales. On average, overcontrolled children received higher scores than resilient children for problem subscales associated with internalization (Anxiety/Depression, Dependency, Withdrawal/Conflict). To assess the reliability of these differences, a separate multiple regression analysis was conducted for the total problem score and for each of the six subtype problem scores. Dummy variables were used to represent the contrast of the overcontrolled type (coded 1) with the resilient type (the other two groups coded as 0) and for the comparison of the undercontrolled type with the resilient type (undercontrolled coded as 1, the other two groups coded as 0). Table 2 presents the results of this analysis. Undercontrolled

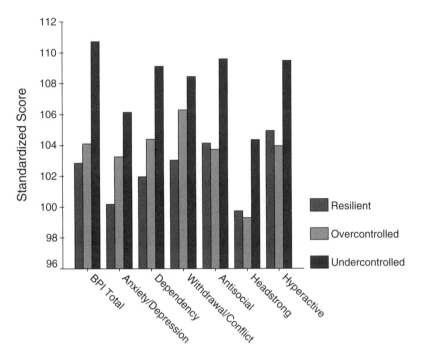

FIGURE 2.—Age 6 mean Behavior Problem Index (BPI) total score and subscale scores for the resilient, overcontrolled, and undercontrolled personality types.

children were significantly higher on all seven scores than were resilient children. This may reflect the lack of differentiation among the subtype problem scores noted earlier. Overcontrolled children were significantly higher than resilient children on the three measures associated with internalization, but not on the total problem index or on the other subtype problem scores.

To summarize, the association of behavior problems with personality type is generally consistent with our hypotheses. However, the relation of behavior problems as judged by mothers and personality type was relatively weak. This may be a consequence of the fact that maternal ratings of subtype problems are not independent of each other.

Behavior ratings. The six behavior ratings of the child made by the researcher were analyzed with a principal components analysis. Two principal components with eigenvalues greater than 1 were identified. Table 3 presents the findings from this analysis. The first principal component, which we labeled *Engagement*, corresponds to ratings about attitude toward being tested, rapport with the interviewer, persistence,

30

TABLE 3

Factor Loadings (following varimax rotation) from Principal-Components Analysis of Behavior Ratings of 6-Year-Olds: Communalities, Eigenvalues, and Percentages of Variance

	Factor		Communalities
	1	2	
Engagement			
Attitude toward being tested	.91	−.22	.87
Rapport with interviewer	.91	−.17	.86
Perseverance/persistence	.90	−.16	.83
Cooperation	.84	−.33	.80
Motivation/interest	.87	−.25	.82
Shy/Anxious			
Shyness/anxiety at the beginning	−.14	.91	.85
Shyness/anxiety at the end	−.30	.85	.81
Eigenvalues	4.69	1.16	
Percentage of variance	66.96	16.61	

cooperation, and motivation. The second principal component is constituted of the two ratings of *Shy/Anxious* behavior. We used factor scores (regression method) for each component as a summary measure. To ease comparison between the two measures, we set the standard deviation at 15 and the mean at 100 for each measure, and then reversed scores for the Engagement measure and relabeled it *Disengagement*. Figure 3 presents the mean scores for disengaged and shy/anxious for the three personality types. Consonant with expectations, the resilient type was lower than the other two types on both measures. The overcontrolled group had the highest score for shy/anxious, the undercontrolled type had the highest mean for disengagement. The mean differences between personality types were small, generally less than one-fourth of a standard deviation. Nonetheless, the differences were statistically reliable, as the regression results in Table 4 indicate.

DISCUSSION

In this study, three distinct personality types were identified using maternal personality ratings of 6-year-old children. Three very similar types were identified in seven subsamples, each with hundreds of children, suggesting that the types are replicable. Finally, the personality types identified in this study have clear conceptual parallels to personality types

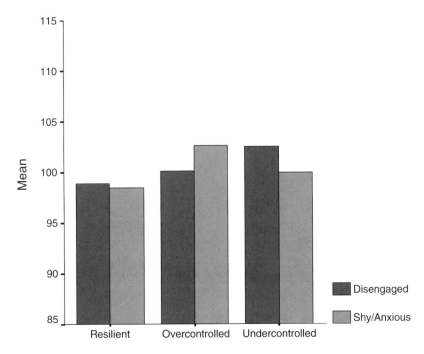

FIGURE 3.—Age 6 mean scores for Disengagement and Shy/Anxious by personality type.

TABLE 4

MULTIPLE REGRESSION RESULTS FOR EQUATIONS PREDICTING BEHAVIOR RATING SCORES

	Resilient (0)/ Overcontrolled (1) Contrast			Resilient (0)/ Undercontrolled (1) Contrast			R for equation
	B	SEB	Beta	B	SEB	Beta	
Disengaged	.05	.05	.02	.23	.06	.09*	.09
Shy/Anxious	.26	.05	.12*	.09	.06	.04	.11

Note.—There were 1848 participants for each of the reported equations.
*$p < .05$.

identified in other studies using Q-sort data. Although other studies identifying types have reported replication analyses in one or two subsamples of populations of children judged to be at risk (Robins et al., 1996) or living in small rural Icelandic villages (Hart et al., 1997), this is the first study to report robust replication of types in a national sample. We

32

conclude that 6-year-old children in the United States can be reliably assigned to one of three personality types.

What does assignment to a personality type imply for childhood functioning? Findings in this study suggest that personality types have associations with achievement, maternal ratings of problems, and behavior ratings made by researchers. Children who are undercontrolled perform less well on an objective measure of academic achievement than do resilient children, and are judged by interviewers to be less engaged in the testing context than resilient children. Overcontrolled children were judged by interviewers to be shyer than children in the resilient category. Together, these findings demonstrate that the personality types identified in this study are grounded in children's thinking and behavior, and are not merely mental models of American mothers.

Findings from this study demonstrate that personality types can be identified in a diverse sample of 6-year-old American children and that these types are associated in sensible ways with measures of academic achievement and behavior. Together, these findings begin to lay the foundation for a person-centered approach to the intersection of personality and childhood development—the aim of this *Monograph*.

Many questions remain, of course. One important issue not addressed by the findings in this chapter is whether the same personality types can be identified in children who are younger or older than 6 years of age, the age cohort of the sample in this study. Certainly a personality typology would have limited value for developmentalists if it were only applicable to 6-year-old children, with radically different types characterizing the trait profiles of children older and younger than age 6. We address this issue in the next chapter.

Second, although the constitution of the types was replicated in seven subsamples in this study, we have only the set of findings for the entire sample to estimate the magnitude of the associations of types to achievement and behavior. The magnitude of these associations is important for our understanding of the nature of the types. In this study, the magnitude of associations suggests that personality type is meaningfully related to achievement and behavior, but not identical with either. If the magnitude of associations were substantially lower than what we observed in this study, then a claim for an organizing role of personality type in development would be undermined, as there would be essentially no relation between personality type and cognition or behavior. Similarly, if the magnitude of associations were much higher, then the conceptual independence of the types from cognition and behavior is called into question. In chapter III, we seek to replicate the associations of personality type to academic achievement and behavior, as accurate estimates of the magnitude of these associations sharpen our understanding of personality types.

Finally, a number of important questions concerning stability and change in personality type, the impact of personality type on development, and the associations of contexts of development with changes in personality type cannot be answered with the cross-sectional analyses reported in this study. These questions are explored through longitudinal analyses in chapters IV–VI.

III. REPLICATION WITH 5-YEAR-OLDS OF TYPES AND THEIR ASSOCIATIONS WITH ACHIEVEMENT AND BEHAVIOR

Fundamental to the notion of scientific progress is the accumulation of replications. A theory or hypothesis that has been tested on multiple occasions and has received confirming support is considered better established than a theory or hypothesis for which evidence has been accrued in only a single study (Laudan, 1990). Although the importance of replication studies has long been recognized by methodologists (e.g., Campbell & Stanley, 1963), the advent of meta-analysis, with its new tools for the integration of replication studies, has resulted in deepened appreciation for the value of multiple studies with similar measures (e.g., Schmidt, 1992).

Replications come in many flavors. Hunter (2001) has proposed a threefold typology of replications: *statistical, scientific,* and *conceptual*. Statistical replications are studies that exactly duplicate another: identical measures, samples, and so forth. The value of statistical replications is that they lead to greater precision in the estimation of effect sizes than is possible from a single study alone. Scientific replications, of which the study reported in this chapter is an example, use the same procedures and assess the same variables as the original study, but may use different measures of the variables and an equivalent but different population. The differences in measures and in populations between a scientific replication and the original target study contribute to an understanding of the generalizability and external validity (Rosenthal, 1990) of the original study's findings. Conceptual replications resemble scientific replications, except that conceptual replications add conditions or variables that are intended to test the possibility that the effects observed in the original study are better explained by the new manipulation or variable than they were by the network of theory and constructs offered in the target study.

As Rosenthal (1990) has pointed out, all too often the replication of findings has been interpreted to mean that effect sizes for parallel variables in two studies are reliably different from zero. Such an interpretation leads to mistaken inferences. For example, if the beta weight for the resilient/ undercontrolled contrast in the prediction of academic achievement is .10 in the original study and .90 in the replication, the contrast is significantly greater than zero in both cases but the two findings are so different as to lead to completely different interpretations. A beta weight of .10 suggests a weak relationship of personality to achievement; a beta weight of .90 suggests that personality and academic achievement are essentially indistinguishable. Consequently, even though the effects in this hypothetical example are represented by beta weights that are both greater than zero, we would not infer that the findings from the second study replicate those of the first.

Replication of findings only occurs when a set of findings from one study deepens the support for an empirical pattern in another study. This requires a direct comparison of the magnitude of effect sizes in the replication studies with those in the target study. If the effect sizes in the replication study are similar to those in the original study, then the findings replicate. Rosenthal (1990) suggested several techniques for assessing the similarity of effect sizes for parallel variables. We adapted one of these techniques, the *replication plane*, for use in this study. A replication plane is a scatter plot of effect sizes for parallel variables in two studies. If one study truly replicates the findings of another, the effect sizes must be similar, as suggested by points in the scatter plot that are on or close to the diagonal. A failure to replicate is suggested by effect sizes for parallel variables with very different magnitudes, evident in a scatter plot with points quite distant from the diagonal.

In this study we use a replication plane to assess similarity in effect sizes reported in chapter II and in this chapter for the relation of the resilient/ overcontrolled contrast to academic achievement and behavior ratings. A replication plane is also used to depict the relation of effect sizes reported in these chapters for the relation of the resilient/undercontrolled contrast and its correlates. Our prediction was that the effects sizes in both planes will be close to the diagonal, suggesting that the results reported in this chapter replicate those reported in chapter II.

The goal here was to replicate the main findings of chapter II with a younger sample. The measures and analytic approach reported in chapter II are used in this chapter, but the chapter II study was of 6-year-olds and for this replication study we made use of the 5-year-olds in the NLSY data set (these are samples of different individuals, not the same sample measured at two time points). We proceeded in two steps. First, we conducted analyses parallel to those in chapter II, seeking to test four hypotheses:

1. The personality typology of resilient, overcontrolled, and under-controlled can be identified in 5-year-olds.

2.   The undercontrolled type is lower than the other two types on a standardized measure of academic achievement.

3.   Children of the overcontrolled type are more likely than children of the other two types to be characterized as having problems with internalization, and children of the undercontrolled type are more likely than resilient or overcontrolled children to be viewed as externalizing.

4.   Overcontrolled children are shyer than resilient children and undercontrolled children are less engaged than resilient children in a testing situation.

In the second step, we used replication planes to test another hypothesis:

5.   The effect sizes obtained in this study are similar in magnitude to the effect sizes reported in the chapter II study.

METHOD

Participants

Participants in the replication study were those children who were 5 years old at one of seven testing times (1986, 1988, 1990, 1992, 1994, 1996, 1998) and for whom maternal ratings were available for each of the 20 personality items. Of the 3033 participants (51% male), 20% were Hispanic, 28% were Black, and 52% were White.

Measures

Measures of personality, cognition, behavior problems, and behavior were identical to those used in the study reported in chapter II. All assessments were made when the children were 5 years old.

RESULTS

Identification of Types

The personality types identified among the 5-year-olds were highly similar to those found among the 6-year-olds. Personality types were constructed following the procedures described in chapter II. Participants were randomly assigned to one of seven subsamples. For each subsample, we conducted an inverse factor analysis (principal components analysis, with a three-component solution and varimax rotation specified) of the maternal personality ratings. The vector of factor scores for the first factor in one solution was then correlated with the vector of factor scores for all other factors in each of the other solutions; the same procedure was followed with the vectors of scores for the second and third factors. These correlations are presented in Appendix B. The convergence correlations are those for the same factor from different samples. Most of convergence correlations were greater than .80, indicating substantial convergence in factors across the seven subsamples.

As in the original study of 6-year-olds, each of the 5-year-old participant's factor loadings were used to assign participants to preliminary personality prototypes. Participants were assigned to preliminary proto- types if (a) their factor loading was equal to or greater than .4, (b) their second highest factor loading score was .2 less than the highest score, and (c) at least one factor loading score was less than .4. Following the procedure described in chapter II, cluster analysis was used to assign all participants to prototypes using uniform rules. The initial starting point for the cluster analysis was determined by calculating average scores for the 20 standardized personality ratings for all participants assigned to each preliminary prototype. The means for the 20 standardized personality ratings for each preliminary prototype were used as initial starting points for a k-means cluster analysis (SPSS quick cluster routine, with a 3-cluster solution specified). The cluster analysis procedure resulted in the assign- ment of each participant to one cluster (or personality prototype).

To assess the similarity of the three personality types derived in this study with the types independently derived in the study of 6-year-olds, the vector of mean standardized scores for the 20 resilient personality items for the resilient type derived in the 5-year-olds was correlated with the corresponding vector for the 6-year-olds; similarly, correlations were calculated for vectors for the overcontrolled types at ages 5 and 6 and vectors for the undercontrolled types at the two ages. All three correlations exceeded .97, demonstrating that the independently derived personality types for the 5-year-olds were essentially indistinguishable from those found for the 6-year-olds.

Some participants included in the derivation of types had siblings who were also in the sample. This kind of relation between participants violates the assumptions of the statistical analyses that follow. Consequently, as in the original study, we included only the oldest participant in each family.

In this replication study, 1068 (47%) of the children were assigned to the resilient type (46% of the girls), 714 (32%) to the overcontrolled type (34% of the girls), and 470 (20%) to the undercontrolled type (20% of the girls). The association between type and gender was statistically reliable ($\chi^2 = 6.02, p < .05$).

Academic Achievement

The association of academic achievement with personality type for the 5-year-olds had the same pattern reported in chapter II for 6-year-olds: On average, resilient children had the highest scores, followed by over-controlled children, then undercontrolled children (with means of 104.7, 103.8, and 99.7, respectively; for the sample, the mean was 103.4, $SD = 12.9$). A multiple regression analysis confirmed the reliability of the difference between those assigned to the resilient type and those of the undercontrolled type (undercontrolled contrast: $B = -5.09$, $SE = .73$, $\beta = -.16$, $p < .01$; overcontrolled contrast: $B = -.93$, $SE = .64$, $\beta = -.03$; $R = .15$, $N = 2127$).

Behavior Ratings

Behavior problems. Following the procedure outlined in chapter II, we used scores on the Depression/Anxiety scale and the Antisocial scale as measures of internalizing and externalizing behavior, respectively. Each scale has a mean of 100 and a standard deviation of 15 in the national norming sample. Participants with internalizing (Depression/Anxiety) scores above 112 (approximately the 80th percentile in the norming sample) and externalizing (Antisocial) scores below 112 were assigned to the internalizing group. Those with externalizing scores greater than or equal to 112 and scores less than 112 on the internalizing measure were assigned to the externalizing group. Participants with scores equal to or greater than 112 on both scales were assigned to the multiproblem group, and those with scores lower than 112 on both scores were categorized in the no problem group.

Figure 4 presents the percentage of resilient, overcontrolled, and undercontrolled participants assigned to each of the four problem groups. The association of personality type with diagnostic group (defined following the procedure described in chapter II) was significant (χ^2 [2201] = 112.86, $p < .01$). The pattern of association for the 5-year-olds was consistent with that found for the 6-year-olds, as reported in chapter II, with 10% of overcontrolled children, but only 5% of the resilient and 7% of the undercontrolled children, assigned to the internalizing group. Twenty-eight percent of the undercontrolled children were classified in the externalizing group, higher than the rates for the resilient (26%) and undercontrolled (17%) types.

Figure 5 depicts the average scores for total behavior problems and each of the six problem subscales for the three personality types. As reported in chapter II, undercontrolled children had the highest average scores for total problems and for all six subtype problem subscales. On

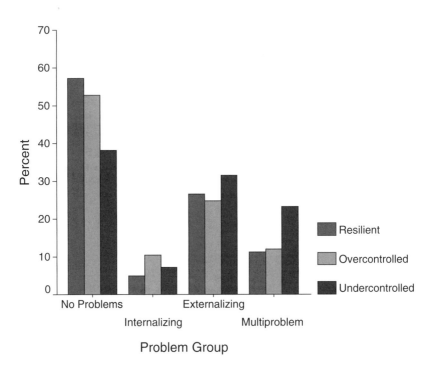

FIGURE 4.—Percentage of 5-year-old participants of each personality type in each problem group.

average, overcontrolled children received higher scores than resilient children for problem subscales associated with internalization (Anxiety/Depression, Dependency). To assess the reliability of these differences, a separate multiple regression analysis was conducted for the total problem score and for each of the six subtype problem scores. Dummy variables were used to represent the contrast of the overcontrolled type (coded 1) with the resilient type (the other two groups coded as 0) and for the comparison of the undercontrolled type with the resilient type (undercontrolled coded as 1, the other two groups coded as 0). Table 5 presents the results of this analysis. Undercontrolled children were significantly higher on all seven scores than were resilient children. This may reflect the lack of differentiation among the subtype problem scores noted in chapter II. Overcontrolled children were significantly higher than resilient children on the three measures associated with internalization, but not on the total problem index or on the other subtype problem scores.

Observer ratings of behavior. The six behavior ratings of the child made by the researcher were analyzed with a principal components analysis.

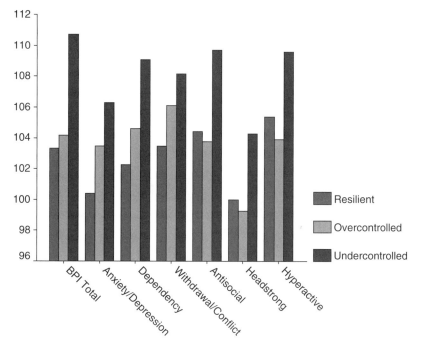

FIGURE 5.—Age 5 mean Behavior Problem Index (BPI) total score and subscale scores for the resilient, overcontrolled, and undercontrolled personality types.

Two principal components with eigenvalues greater than 1 were identified. Table 6 presents the findings from this analysis. The first principal component (Engagement) corresponds to ratings about attitude, rapport with the interviewer, persistence, cooperation, and motivation, as was the case in chapter II. The second principal component is composed of the two ratings of Shy/Anxious behavior. We used factor scores (regression method) for each component as a summary measure. To ease comparison between the two measures, we set the standard deviation at 15 and the mean at 100 for each measure, and then reversed scores for the engagement measure, and relabeled it *Disengagement*. Figure 6 presents the mean scores for disengaged and shy/anxious for the three personality types. Table 7 presents the results of the regression analyses testing the reliability of the differences among personality types. Consonant with expectations, the resilient type was lower than the other two types on both measures. The overcontrolled group had the highest score for shy/anxious, the undercontrolled type had the highest mean for disengagement. The mean differences between personality types were small, generally less than one fourth of a standard deviation. Nonetheless, the differences are statistically reliable.

41

TABLE 5

MULTIPLE REGRESSION RESULTS FOR EQUATIONS PREDICTING BEHAVIOR PROBLEM TOTAL SCORE AND SUBSCALE SCORES

Behavior Problem	Resilient (0)/ Overcontrolled (1) Contrast			Resilient (0)/ Undercontrolled (1) Contrast			R for equation	M for Sample	SD for Sample
	B	SEB	Beta	B	SEB	Beta			
Total Score	.77	.76	.02	7.49	.87	.21*	.20	104.67	14.74
Anxiety/Depression	2.83	.66	.10*	6.06	.76	.19*	.18	102.52	13.22
Dependency	2.14	.67	.07*	6.83	.77	.20*	.19	104.78	13.77
Peer withdrawal/Conflict	2.30	.68	.08*	4.72	.77	.14*	.14	104.75	12.82
Antisocial	-.68	.70	-.02	5.46	.80	.16*	.17	104.88	13.65
Headstrong	-.72	.66	-.03	4.39	.76	.13*	.15	100.77	12.38
Hyperactive	-1.39	.72	-.04	4.33	.82	.12*	.14	105.06	14.11

Note.—There were 2193 and 2259 participants for each of the reported equations.

*$p < .05$.

42

TABLE 6

FACTOR LOADINGS (FOLLOWING VARIMAX ROTATION) FROM PRINCIPAL-COMPONENTS ANALYSIS OF BEHAVIOR RATINGS OF 5-YEAR-OLDS: COMMUNALITIES, EIGENVALUES, AND PERCENTAGES OF VARIANCE

	Factor		
	1	2	Communalities
Engagement			
Attitude toward being tested	.91	−.21	.87
Rapport with interviewer	.91	−.19	.87
Perseverance/persistence	.91	−.15	.84
Cooperation	.83	−.34	.81
Motivation/interest	.86	−.29	.83
Shy/Anxious			
Shyness/anxiety at the beginning	−.14	.91	.85
Shyness/anxiety at the end	−.32	.84	.80
Eigenvalues	4.73	1.13	
Percentage of variance	67.15	16.16	

Assessment of Replication of Findings

The pattern of significance of effects for the personality types in this replication study was similar to that found in the original study (chapter II). However, as discussed at the beginning of this chapter, the replication of findings is best judged by comparing the magnitude of effects for parallel variables in the two studies. Our prediction was that the effects in the two studies would be very similar. In each study, 10 beta weights were calculated for the effect of the resilient/overcontrolled contrast: 1 for the prediction of achievement, 6 subscales scores and 1 total score for the Behavior Problem Index, and 2 scores for the Behavior ratings. Each study also has 10 beta weights, corresponding to effect sizes, for the resilient/undercontrolled contrast. As the extent of replication of findings depends on the similarity of the effects in the original study to the parallel effects in the replication study, we constructed two plots, or replication planes (Rosenthal, 1990), one for the effects involving the resilient/overcontrolled contrast and the other for the resilient/undercontrolled plot. The points in Plot A in Figure 7 are the 10 beta weights for the resilient/overcontrolled contrast. For example, one point in the plot corresponds to the beta weight for the resilient/ overcontrolled reported in chapter II for the prediction of academic achievement and the parallel beta weight in this replication study.

Replication of findings is indicated by similar effect sizes, which in turn is demonstrated by the points in a replication plane falling on the diagonal (Rosenthal, 1990). It is evident from Plot A that the effect sizes for the

43

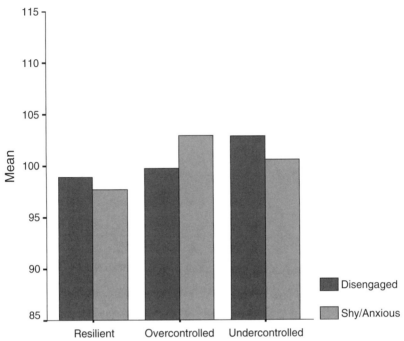

FIGURE 6.—Age 5 mean scores for Disengagement and Shy/Anxious by personality type.

TABLE 7

MULTIPLE REGRESSION RESULTS FOR EQUATIONS PREDICTING BEHAVIOR RATING SCORES

	Resilient (0)/ Overcontrolled (1) Contrast			Resilient (0)/ Undercontrolled (1) Contrast			
	B	SEB	Beta	B	SEB	Beta	R for equation
Disengaged	.06	.05	.03	.25	.06	.11*	.10
Shy/Anxious	.38	.05	.18*	.20	.06	.08*	.17

Note.—There were 2108 participants for each of the reported equations.
*p < .05.

original study of 6-year-olds and the effect sizes for the resilient/over-controlled contrast are very similar—are very close to the diagonal—and consequently we conclude that the study reported in here replicates closely the study presented in chapter II concerning the resilient/overcontrolled contrast.

Plot B in Figure 7 illustrates the relation of beta weights in the original study of 6-year-olds with the corresponding beta weights in this study of 5-year-olds for the resilient/undercontrolled contrast. Again, the replication

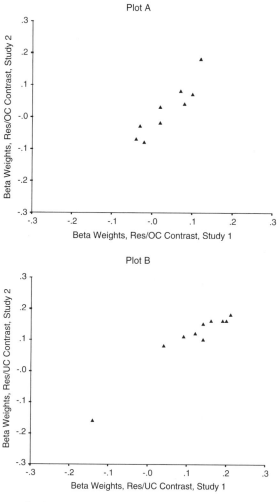

FIGURE 7.—Replication plots. Note that in Figure 7a two points have the same coordinates. (Res = resilient personality type, OC = overcontrolled personality type, UC = undercontrolled personality type.)

plot suggests that the effect sizes are very similar for the two studies, indicating that the findings reported here replicate the findings reported in chapter II.

DISCUSSION

The study with 5-year-olds reported here provides powerful replication support for the personality types, and their associations with academic

45

achievement and behavior, reported in chapter II in which 6-year-olds constituted the participant pool.

First, the study of 5-year-olds found robust evidence in seven subsamples for three personality types. The mean scores for the 20 personality items for each of the three types are nearly perfectly correlated (all r's greater than .95) with the mean scores for the corresponding type in the original study. This means that between the two studies, in 14 samples of children, three personality types could be identified in maternal personality ratings.

Second, the study of 5-year-olds replicates the findings for 6-year-olds concerning the relation of personality type to academic achievement, behavior problems, and behavior ratings. In both studies, in comparison to resilient children, overcontrolled children were judged to be higher in dependency, anxiety/depression, and shyness. Similarly, both studies found that undercontrolled children, when compared with resilient children, are lower in academic achievement, all six subtypes of behavior problems, total behavior problems, and disengagement. This pattern of findings demonstrates again that the personality types have relations to academic achievement and behavior that are consistent with findings in previous work.

Third, the replication planes indicate that the magnitude of associations of personality type to academic achievement and behavior varies little across the two populations studied. The consistency of effect sizes across the two studies deepens our confidence that the connections among constructs, and the relative strengths of these connections, should be explored for their psychological and social policy implications. In the next chapter, we explore the implications of personality type for academic growth and decline—a line of research suggested by the consistent cross-sectional relation of type and academic achievement found in this chapter and in chapter II.

IV. PERSONALITY TYPES AND ACADEMIC ACHIEVEMENT

In this chapter, we investigate the relation of personality type to growth and decline in academic achievement assessed over time. The general premise underlying this study was that personality, represented in this *Monograph* by the construct of personality type, is associated with the rate of development of psychological phenomena.

Theoretically, the effect of personality type on developmental growth likely occurs through multiple paths. For example, consider the characteristics of those assigned to the resilient personality type as identified in chapters II and III. A resilient child is relatively free of social anxiety, interacts effectively with adults, and focuses attention and engages fully in cognitively demanding situations (this characterization draws on the maternal personality ratings, behavior problems subscales, and interviewer behavior ratings). The resilient child is well prepared to gain new knowledge about the world. He/she can learn effectively from others, as neither social anxiety nor aggression interferes with the social interactions that are central to the construction of knowledge about the social (Piaget, 1932/1965) and physical (Phelps & Damon, 1989) worlds. Moreover, the resilient child is able to focus attention, and consequently is able to attend to the complexities of problems and perspectives that must be analyzed, accepted or rejected, and synthesized with existing concepts and theories in order for more complex understandings to emerge.

Neither the overcontrolled nor undercontrolled child can be expected to benefit as much in transactions with the world. The overcontrolled child—shy, dependent, prone to negative emotions—is likely to have a more restricted range of social relationships than the resilient child. Moreover, the overcontrolled child's tendency to anxiety may result in withdrawal from challenging social interactions and learning contexts that pose the risk of failure (Hart, Hoffman, & Edelstein, 1996).

Similarly, the undercontrolled child's disengagement in task situations and heightened tendency to aggression probably diminish the benefits derived from social interactions and learning contexts. If undercontrolled children are less prepared to engage successfully in social interaction and to participate fully in cognitively challenging tasks, they should be less likely than children of the other two types to derive benefit from school.

To date, the research evidence is mixed for our hypothesis concerning personality type and academic achievement. In several cross-sectional studies undercontrolled children were found to have lower IQ scores and grade point averages than resilient and overcontrolled children (e.g., Asendorpf and van Aken 1999; Hart et al. 1997; Robins et al. 1996). This pattern was replicated, as reported in chapters II and III. These findings are consistent with our hypothesis that, on average, undercontrolled children learn at a slower rate than other children. In longitudinal studies (Asendorpf and van Aken 1999; Hart et al. 1997) with two small samples (fewer than 40 participants) of undercontrolled children, no significant differences were found between undercontrolled children and other children in their rate of academic development. However, these findings may simply be a reflection of low statistical power due to small sample sizes rather than an indication of no relationship. One goal for the research presented in this chapter was to determine if personality type is associated with children's rate of academic achievement, using two large samples that ensure sufficient statistical power.

We attempted to clarify the distinctive relation of personality type to intellectual development by controlling for other variables that might account for an association between personality and academic growth and decline. First, we included in the analysis frequently studied correlates of academic achievement, including family income, maternal education, quality of the home environment, and ethnicity. Each of these variables is known from previous research to be related to academic achievement, and consequently it is essential to control for them while searching for the unique connection of personality type to academic achievement (see Jencks & Phillips, 1998, for demonstrations of the relevance of these variables in the prediction of academic achievement).

Second, and particularly important for elucidating the role of personality in academic growth, we controlled for the association of *behavior problems* and *self-perceived academic competence* on academic growth. Consider first the role of behavior problems in academic development. It might be argued that a correlation between personality and academic trajectory is wholly a consequence of behavior problems that both cause academic difficulties and result in assignment to the undercontrolled type. For example, a child whose behavior is characterized by problems resulting from distractibility might have trouble learning in school and may be perceived as belonging to the undercontrolled type. In such a case, the relation of personality type to academic growth would be fully *mediated* (Baron & Kenny, 1986) by behavior problems, and explanatory primacy for theory and for intervention might be accorded to behavior problems rather than to personality type.

Similarly, Hair and Graziano (in press) suggested that the relation of personality traits to academic growth and decline is mediated by *self-perceived academic and social competence*. Hair and Graziano found that the personality traits of agreeableness and openness to experience, and self-perceived academic and social competence, are all correlated with changes in academic achievement in high school. Based on their path analyses, Hair and Graziano concluded that the influence of personality traits on academic achievement is largely indirect; the traits predict to self-perceived academic and social competence, which in turn seems to be directly linked to change in academic achievement.

In this chapter, we have hypothesized that personality type is likely related to academic achievement through many paths: the breadth of social relations, the focusing of attention in cognitively challenging situations, emotion regulation, and so forth. Consequently, our prediction is that the relation of personality type to academic development is *not* fully mediated by behavior problems or by self-perceived academic competence. By including measures of problem behaviors and self-perceived academic competence in the analyses, the unique contribution of personality type, independent of behavior problems and self-perceived academic competence, can be assessed.

We assessed growth and decline using *growth curve analysis* (Willett, 1988) to characterize longitudinally assessed achievement. Growth curve analysis involves estimating a curve to represent each participant's developmental trajectory in a particular domain. In the research that follows, a regression line is fit to represent each participant's academic achievement scores at ages 6, 8, 10, and 12 years (Sample 1) or at ages 5, 7, 9, and 11 years (Sample 2). The line allows the participant's scores to be characterized by an *intercept* and a *slope*. The intercept represents the composite level of a participant's standing on a particular variable. The slope indicates whether a participant's standing on a particular variable increases or decreases over the measurement period. It is the slope that indicates growth and decline, and consequently it is the slope that is of central interest here. In the analyses below, we examined whether personality type is related to the slope of each participant's academic achievement measured over a six-year period.

Third, we compare the relative value of personality types and personality traits for the prediction of the rate of academic achievement over the course of childhood. As discussed in chapter 1, some researchers have claimed that personality types allow for better longitudinal predictions than do personality traits because the former incorporate correlations among traits that are not represented in single traits (e.g., Asendorpf & van

Aken, 1999). Other researchers suggest that better predictions can be made with traits, for which scale scores range quantitatively, than from type scores (e.g., Costa et al., 2002). In this chapter we compare predictions of the rate of academic achievement made with personality types to the predictions of the rate of academic achievement made with two traits, *compliance* and *secure attachment*. These two traits are derived from the same personality items that are the basis for the personality types. Our hypothesis was predictions made with personality types are more powerful than predictions made on the basis of two distinct personality traits.

To reiterate, our hypotheses were:

1. In comparison to resilient children, overcontrolled and under-controlled children decline in academic performance over childhood.

2. The relation of personality type to academic performance is partially independent of the effects of problem behavior and self-perceived academic competence on academic growth.

3. Better predictions of the rate of academic achievement over the course of childhood can be made with personality types than with personality traits.

METHOD

Participants

The participants for Sample 1 were the subsample of participants in chapter II who were 6 years old in 1986, 1988, 1990, or 1992. For these participants, subsequent testing times furnished academic achievement data for an additional six years (e.g., a 6-year-old in 1992 was also tested at ages 8, 10, and 12 in 1994, 1996, and 1998 respectively). Moreover, only participants with academic achievement scores (described below) at age 6 and age 12 were included (thus participants with missing scores at either of these ages were omitted).

The participants in Sample 2 were a similarly constituted subsample of participants in chapter III.

Measures

Personality type, ages 5 and 6. Personality type was determined following the procedures described in chapters II and III.

Academic achievement, ages 6–12 (Sample 1) and 5–11(Sample 2). Approximately every two years, participants who were between ages 5 and 12 were administered three subtests of the Peabody Individual

Achievement Test. This means that participants who were assigned to a personality type at age 6 (chapter II) were retested with the Peabody subtests at ages 8, 10, and 12 years. The standard scores for the three subtests (standard scores were based on a 1969 norming sample for the Peabody) were averaged to form an index of academic achievement for each age (this is the same index formed for age 6 academic achievement; the alpha for these composites were .86 for age 8, .84 for age 10, and .85 for age 12). Similarly, participants in Sample 2 were retested with the Peabody subtests at ages 7, 9, and 11 years. The scores for the three subtests were averaged to constitute an index of academic achievement (the alphas for these composites were, respectively, .84, .85, and .83).

For each participant, a regression line—a growth curve—was estimated to represent the relation of academic achievement to age. For greater precision, age in months at the time of the administration of the Peabody was used in the equation, although as we noted the intervals between administrations were approximately two years, and corresponded to ages 6, 8, 10, and 12 years or 5, 7, 9, and 11 years. A positive slope for the regression line suggested that a child's rate of academic achievement, relative to others, was increasing, and a negative slope indicated that a child's rate of academic achievement was slower than that of others. It was the slope indicating academic growth and decline over the age range of 6 to 12 (Sample 1) or 5 to 11 (Sample 2) that was the dependent measure in the analyses that follow.

Home environment, age 5 or 6. The quality of the child's home environment at age 5 or 6 was assessed with the Home Observation Measurement of the Environment–Short Form (HOME-SF, alpha = .73 as reported in the NLSY Handbook; Baker et al., 1993), which combines maternal ratings of the home with ratings made by a trained researcher. In the analyses below, we used a total score standardized on participants in the NLSY with a mean of 100 and a standard deviation of 15. The mean for Sample 1 was 98 ($SD = 15.2$) and for Sample 2 was 98 ($SD = 15$).

Demographics, age 5 or 6. An extensive interview with each mother elicited information concerning her child's health, social, educational histories, and ethnicity; mothers also answered questions concerning family income and maternal educational attainment. For Sample 1 the average family income was \$29,931 ($SD = \$64,063$) and the average maternal educational attainment in years of completed school was 12.1 ($SD = 1.9$). For Sample 2 the average family income was \$29,845 ($SD = \$65,690$) and the mean educational attainment was 12.1 ($SD = 1.9$).

Personality traits, age 5 or 6. As described in chapter II, mothers rated their children on 20 personality items (these are the items in Table 1). Factor analyses of these items have been conducted by several teams of researchers (this research is reviewed by Baydar, 1995), and two dimensions, *compliance* and *insecure attachment*, have been identified. A compliance score has been constructed for the six items reflecting the child's willingness to meet expectations (e.g., "Eats food given," "Turns off TV when told without protest"). The insecure attachment score is the sum of seven items reflecting negative emotions and clinginess in the relationship with the mother (e.g., "Cries when left alone," "Demanding and impatient when mother is busy"). The alphas for these two measures are, respectively, .59 and .52 (Baker et al., 1993).

Problem behaviors, age 11 or 12. As noted in chapters II and III, mothers rated their children at ages 5 and 6 on the Behavior Problem Index (BPI), a 28-item questionnaire tapping common problems of childhood (e.g., "disobedient in school"). Mothers also used the BPI to record their judgments of their children's behavior problems at ages 11 and 12. We used the standardized total score (Sample 1: $M = 107.7$, $SD = 14.2$; Sample 2: $M = 107.4$, $SD = 15.1$).

Self-perceived academic competence, age 12. Self-perceived academic competence was assessed in participants 8 years old and older from 1986–1994. Beginning in 1996, only participants 12 years old and older received these questions. This change in design resulted from concerns about the reliability and validity of the measure for those younger than age 12 (Center for Human Resource Research, 1997). Because scores were consistently available only for those participants ages 12 and older, this variable was included in analyses of Sample 1, but not in analyses of Sample 2 in which participants at the last measurement point were 11 years old.

The measure consists of six questions concerning participants' perceptions of their own academic competence. These questions were slightly modified versions of items from Harter's (1985) scale, and asked children to judge for themselves on a 4-point scale the descriptiveness of statements such as "Some kids feel that they are very good at their school work." Scores for the six items were summed to form the index of self-perceived academic competence. The alpha reliability for this measure in the NLSY was .69 (Baker et al., 1993). For Sample 1, the mean was 17.4 ($SD = 4.23$).

RESULTS

The analyses for Sample 1 are presented first, followed by those for Sample 2.

Sample 1

Attrition. The effects of attrition were tested by comparing those for whom relevant scores are available both when the participants were 6 years old (Time 1) and at later ages (717 participants) to those for whom relevant scores were available only at age 6 (352 participants). *T* tests were used to compare the two groups on Time 1 measures of family income, maternal educational attainment, HOME-SF score, and academic achievement. A significant difference was found only for maternal educational attainment, with mothers of participants who had remained in the study having a slightly higher average level of attainment ($M = 12.1$) than mothers of participants for whom complete sets of data were not available ($M = 11.8$; t [1067] $= 2.67, p < .05$).

Prediction of the rate of intellectual growth with a test for mediation by problem behaviors and self-perceived academic competence. The association of personality type with intellectual growth and decline was tested with multiple regression analysis. As in chapters II and III, dummy variables were constructed to represent personality type (overcontrolled was coded 1 for children in this type and 0 for all others, and undercontrolled was coded 1 for undercontrolled children and 0 for the other two types). Dummy variables also were used to represent ethnicity (Hispanic coded 1 for Hispanics and 0 for all others, and Black coded 1 for Blacks and 0 for all others). Family income (the log of income was used, to minimize skew), HOME-SF scores, and maternal educational attainment also were included in the equation as predictors because these variables are known to be associated with academic achievement.

We also tested for the possible mediating effects of age 12 behavior problems and age 12 self-perceived academic competence. For these variables to *mediate* the association of personality type to rate of academic achievement growth, three conditions must be met (Baron & Kenny, 1986). First, age 12 behavior problems and age 12 self-perceived academic competence must be correlated with the rate of academic achievement growth. The correlations of the rate of academic achievement to behavior problems and self-perceived academic competence were, respectively, $-.18$ ($p < .001$) and .27 ($p < .001$), and therefore the first condition for mediation was met.

Second, for statistical mediation there must be an association of personality types to behavior problems and self-perceived academic competence. The three types did differ in age 12 behavior problems (with mean scores of 106.7, 107.6, and 110.5 for resilient, overcontrolled, and undercontrolled, respectively) and age 12 self-perceived academic competence (mean scores for resilient, overcontrolled, and undercontrolled of 17.8, 17.5, and 16.6, respectively). We assessed the reliability of differences in age 12 behavior problems by using multiple regression with dummy codes to represent the three personality types (dummy code for overcontrolled was 1 for children of the overcontrolled type and 0 for the other two; dummy code for undercontrolled was 1 for children of the undercontrolled type and 0 for children of the other two types). Only the dummy variable for the undercontrolled contrast was significant (undercontrolled contrast: $B = 3.76$, $SE = 1.41$, $\beta = .10$, $p < .01$; overcontrolled contrast: $B = .89$, $SE = 1.23$, $\beta = .03$, $p > .10$; $R = .10$, $N = 717$). The parallel analysis with the age 12 self-perceived competence scores yielded similar findings (undercontrolled contrast: $B = -11.52$, $SE = 4.19$, $\beta = -.11$, $p < .01$; overcontrolled contrast: $B = -2.83$, $SE = 3.66$, $\beta = -.03$, $p > .10$; $R = .10$, $N = 717$). These findings demonstrated that personality type measured at age 6 years was a predictor of the behavior problems and self-perceived academic competence assessed at age 12 years.

The final step in the test of mediation was to determine whether the inclusion of the mediators in the regression equation predicting the variable of interest eliminates the association of the original predictors to the outcome variable. The relevant results are presented in Table 8. The left-hand columns of Table 8 present the results of the multiple regression analyses for Sample 1, comprised of the participants who were 6 years old at Time 1. The beta weights for the variables at age 6 of achievement and Black are the largest. Six-year-olds with low age 6 achievement scores developed at a faster rate than children with higher scores, an effect that may reflect both regression to the mean and the compensatory effects of school for children with relatively little opportunity for learning at home. The beta weight for the Black-White contrast suggests that Black children acquire academic knowledge at a slower rate in childhood. This is a well-replicated effect (Phillips, Crouse, & Ralph, 1998) attributable to economic and educational segregation among other factors (for thoughtful discussions, see Jencks & Phillips, 1998).

Turning to the main areas of interest in this *Monograph*, the results in Table 8 suggest that undercontrolled children, relative to resilient children, declined in academic achievement. The contribution of personality type to the prediction of growth and decline was modest. For example, the association of the undercontrolled contrast to the

TABLE 8

PREDICTORS OF RATE (GROWTH CURVE SLOPE) OF ACADEMIC ACHIEVEMENT FOR 6-YEAR-OLDS (SAMPLE 1)

| | Personality Type Analyses | | | | | | Personality Trait Analyses | | | | | |
| | Model 1 | | | Model 2 | | | Model 1 | | | Model 2 | | |
Predictor	B	SEB	Beta	B	SEB	Beta	B	SEB	Beta	B	SEB	Beta
Compliant							.042	.014	.11*	.041	.013	.11
Insecure attachment							.000	.000	.07	.000	.000	.04
Overcontrolled	−.016	.011	−.05	−.012	.011	−.04						
Undercontrolled	−.038	.013	−.10**	−.028	.013	−.08*						
Net family income (log)	.040	.014	.11**	.039	.013	.11**	.009	.003	.12**	.006	.003	.09**
HOME-SF	.000	.000	.08	.000	.000	.04	−.021	.013	−.06	−.022	.013	−.06
Maternal educational attainment	.009	.003	.12**	.007	.003	.09*	−.064	.012	−.21**	−.064	.011	−.21**
Hispanic	−.022	.013	−.06*	−.022	.013	−.06	.004	.010	.01	.002	.009	.01
Black	−.067	.012	−.22**	−.066	.011	−.22**	−.005	.001	−.35**	−.006	.001	−.39**
Gender (0 = male, 1 = female)	.004	.010	.01	.002	.009	.01	.003	.001	.10	.002	.001	.06
Academic achievement, age 6	−.005	.001	−.34**	−.006	.001	−.39**	−.001	.001	−.04**	−.001	.001	−.02**
Behavior problem total score, age 12				−.001	.000	−.11**				−.001	.000	−.11**
Perceived academic competence, age 12				.001	.000	.28**				.001	.000	.28**
R^2 change			.18			.10			.18			.09
F change (717 participants)			16.96**			46.42**			17.18**			44.82**

*$p < .05$;
**$p < .01$.

55

growth curve slope was small (beta = −.10). However, the undercontrolled contrast was as powerful a predictor of intellectual growth and decline as were family income, home environment, maternal educational attainment, and problem behaviors.

Note that in the second analysis, age 12 behavior problems and age 12 self-perceived academic competence were good predictors of the rate of change in academic achievement between ages 6 and 12. Children who were low in behavior problems and high in self-perceived academic competence at age 12 had improved most in academic standing since age 6. Most important for our purposes in this chapter, however, is that there was little indication of mediation on the effect of personality type on academic growth, as the beta weight in the second analysis for the undercontrolled contrast was little different from the corresponding beta weight in the first analysis.

Predictive value of personality types versus personality traits. We conducted parallel analyses using the traits of compliance ($M = 23.35$, $SD = 4.51$) and insecure attachment ($M = 17.96$, $SD = 4.51$) to predict the rate of change in academic achievement. These analyses are presented in the right-hand columns of Table 8. Compliance was a predictor of the rate of academic growth, although the association was weaker than the associations observed with personality types. Moreover, neither compliance nor insecure attachment was a significant predictor of the rate of academic growth once the age 12 behavior problem and the age 12 self-perceived academic competence scores were entered. In summary, the evidence for the 6-year-olds suggested that personality types produced better prediction of the trajectory of academic achievement than did the personality traits of compliance and secure attachment.

Sample 2

A similar set of analyses was conducted with the participants who were 5-years-old at Time 1, except that age 11 self-perceived academic competence was not available for testing as a possible mediator because this measure was not administered to all 11-year-old participants (as discussed in the Method section).

Attrition. There were 837 5-year-old participants with complete data at Time 1 and at subsequent testing points, and 353 for whom complete data were available only for Time 1. *T*-tests were again used to compare those for whom complete data at all testing times were available to those for whom data were available only at age 5 years. A significant difference was found for maternal educational attainment, with mothers of

56

participants who remained in the study with a slightly lower average level of attainment ($M = 12.1$) than mothers of participants for whom complete sets of data were not available ($M = 11.8$, t [1187] $= 2.59$, $p < .05$).

Prediction of the rate of intellectual growth with a test for mediation by problem behaviors. To determine whether age 11 behavior problems could be a potential mediator, the total score was correlated with the slope of academic achievement. The correlation between age 11 behavior problems and the slope was $- .07$, $p < .05$, demonstrating that age 11 behavior problems met one of the conditions necessary for mediation.

Next, the association of age 11 behavior problems to personality type was assessed. Age 11 behavior problems were higher among those of the undercontrolled personality type ($M = 110.9$) than those of the resilient type ($M = 106.3$) or overcontrolled type ($M = 106.5$). To test the significance of this difference, we used multiple regression with dummy codes to represent the three personality types (dummy code for overcontrolled was coded 1 for children of the overcontrolled type and 0 for the other two; dummy code for undercontrolled was coded 1 for children of the undercontrolled type and 0 for children of the other two types). Only the dummy variable for the undercontrolled contrast was significant (undercontrolled contrast: $B = 4.56$, $SE = 1.36$, $\beta = .12$, $p < .01$; overcontrolled contrast: $B = .19$, $SE = 1.19$, $\beta = .01$, $p > .10$; $R = .12$, $N = 837$). From this pattern, we concluded that the behavior problems construct met the second condition of statistical mediation.

Table 9 presents the multiple regression analyses predicting the slope for academic achievement. The left side of the table presents the analyses using personality type as a predictor, and the right side displays the results for the parallel analyses using the personality traits of compliance and insecure attachment. Consider first the analyses with personality types as predictors. Once again, the variable corresponding to the undercontrolled personality type was a significant predictor of a decline in academic achievement over a six-year-span. Moreover, although total score for age 11 behavior problems did predict to the slope of academic achievement development, entering it into the equation had little effect on the predictive value of personality types, as indicated by little difference in the beta weight for the undercontrolled variable in the two analyses. This suggests that the association of personality type to the rate of academic achievement development was not mediated by age 11 behavior problems.

Predictive value of personality types versus personality traits. The right-hand columns of Table 9 present the results of the analyses using the personality trait variables of compliance and insecure attachment.

TABLE 9

PREDICTORS OF RATE (GROWTH CURVE SLOPE) OF ACADEMIC ACHIEVEMENT FOR 5-YEAR-OLDS (SAMPLE 2)

| | Personality Type Analyses | | | | | | Personality Trait Analyses | | | | | |
| | Model 1 | | | Model 2 | | | Model 1 | | | Model 2 | | |
Predictor	B	SEB	Beta	B	SEB	Beta	B	SEB	Beta	B	SEB	Beta
Compliant							.002	.001	.05	.001	.001	.04
Insecure attachment							−.001	.001	−.04	−.001	.001	−.02
Overcontrolled	−.005	.010	−.01	−.004	.010	−.01						
Undercontrolled	−.038	.012	−.10**	−.034	.012	−.09*						
Net family income (log)	.047	.011	.14**	.044	.011	.13**	.048	.011	.14**	.045	.011	.13**
HOME-SF	.000	.000	.10**	.000	.000	.08*	.000	.000	.10**	.000	.000	.08**
Maternal educational attainment	.007	.003	.09**	.007	.003	.08**	.007	.003	.09**	.007	.003	.09**
Hispanic	−.016	.012	−.04	−.021	.012	−.05	−.016	.012	−.04	−.021	.012	−.05
Black	−.058	.011	−.18**	−.061	.011	−.19**	−.059	.011	−.18**	−.063	.011	−.19**
Gender (0 = male, 1 = female)	−.001	.009	.00	−.003	.009	−.01	.000	.009	.00	−.002	.009	−.01
Academic achievement, age 6	−.008	.000	−.63**	−.008	.000	−.63**	−.008	.000	−.63**	−.008	.000	−.63**
Behavior problem total score, age 11				−.001	.000	−.10**				−.001	.000	−.10**
R^2 change			.35			.01			.35			.01
F change (837 participants)			50.35**			12.59**			49.40**			11.90**

*$p < .05$;
**$p < .01$.

Neither compliance nor insecure attachment was a significant predictor of the rate of academic achievement.

Summary Analyses

Together, the analyses for Samples 1 and 2 demonstrate that the undercontrolled personality type was associated with intellectual decline in childhood. Moreover, personality type was as good a predictor of intellectual growth and decline as was family income or the quality of the family environment as reflected with the global HOME-SF score. Third, our results demonstrated that the association of personality with intellectual decline was not mediated by problem behaviors or self-perceived academic competence. Finally, personality types were found to be better predictors of the rate of academic growth than were personality trait measures constructed from the same data used to identify the personality types.

How much decline over the six-year period was associated with personality type? An illustration is provided in Figure 8, which depicts change between ages 6 and 12 on the measure of academic achievement for each of the three personality types (15 points corresponds to 1 *SD* change in scores between ages 6 and 12). The points in the graph were estimated using the regression weights for the personality types from the first regression equation in Table 8, in which the effects of demographic variables were controlled. To illustrate the differences in trajectories, the lines were estimated for White males from families with average incomes at

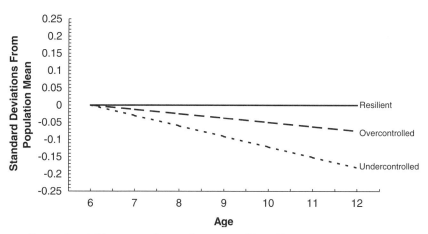

FIGURE 8.—Achievement change for 6-year-old children of each personality type estimated from regression equation. (Values for White males with average family incomes and environments, average level of maternal educational attainment, and average age 6 achievement and behavior problem levels were used to estimate the points in this graph.)

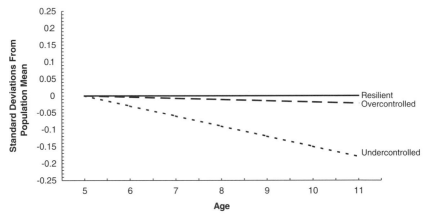

FIGURE 9.—Achievement change for 5-year-old children of each personality type estimated from regression equation. (Values for White males with average family incomes and environments, average level of maternal educational attainment, and average age 5 achievement and behavior problem levels were used to estimate the points in this graph.)

Time 1, and all with achievement scores equal to the population average of 100 at Time 1. The scores were translated into standard deviation units by dividing the estimated achievement scores for each hypothetical individual by 15, the standard deviation for the population. Undercontrolled children declined almost .2 of a standard deviation in academic achievement between ages 6 and 12. Figure 9 depicts the growth trajectories for the 5-year-olds, estimated in the same way.

DISCUSSION

The important finding of this study is that personality types, but not personality traits, are reliably associated with the growth rate of academic achievement over the course of childhood. The evidence is strongest for the link between the undercontrolled type and academic development. In the sample of 6-year-olds at Time 1 and in the sample of 5-year-olds at Time 1, children assigned to the undercontrolled type developed more slowly than children assigned to the resilient type. The association of personality type to academic achievement development is of approximately the same magnitude as the association of home environment, maternal education, or family income to academic achievement development. All of these associations are small, but they are genuinely meaningful for understanding individual differences in development. For example, consider the economic benefits associated with academic achievement as measured on tests such as those used in this study. Winship and Korenman (1999), using the adult sample of the NLSY, found that academic achievement (indexed by the Armed Forces Qualification Test [AFQT], which assesses verbal and mathematical knowledge) measured in late adolescence is predictive of family income a decade later. Winship and Korenman estimated both the effects of cognitive skills on income and the indirect effect of cognitive skills on academic attainment, which in turn contributes to income. Their estimate was that an increase of 1 standard deviation on the AFQT in late adolescence is associated with a 37% increase in family income as a young adult, suggesting that academic achievement has a substantial economic return in adulthood.

Returning to this study, we found that relative to resilient children, undercontrolled children's slower rate of academic development resulted in a deficit of approximately .15 of a standard deviation in achievement during elementary school. We shall assume for this illustration that this deficit neither grows nor diminishes through high school. This leads to the estimate that the undercontrolled individual's .15 disadvantage in academic achievement in late adolescence resulting from a slower rate of development in childhood will result in a family income 5.55% (.15 × 37%) lower than that of the resilient individual. The median annual family income for householders between 25 and 34 was approximately $44,000 in 2000 (DeNavas-Walt, Cleveland, & Roemer, 2001), from which we can infer that the academic achievement disadvantage resulting from slower academic achievement growth of the undercontrolled child translates into an annual income decrement of approximately $2400.

The social policy significance of the difference between undercontrolled and resilient children in academic achievement resulting from different developmental rates can be estimated in another way. Winship and Korenman (1999) estimated that each year of schooling increases academic achievement by .18 of a standard deviation. Recall that in our study the slower rate of development of undercontrolled children results in a .15 standard deviation deficit in academic achievement after six years. Combining these two estimates, we suggest that the deficit in academic achievement accruing over childhood from the undercontrolled personality type is roughly equivalent to missing a year of school. Judged by the effects of school on academic achievement, or the influence of academic achievement on family income, the difference in rate of development between resilient and undercontrolled children is educationally and financially meaningful.

V. STABILITY AND CHANGE IN PERSONALITY TYPES

In the preceding chapters, we demonstrated both that personality types can be identified in 5- and 6-year-old children and that the undercontrolled type is reliably associated with academic decline over the course of childhood. The analyses in this chapter identify precursors to personality types in 5- and 6-year-old children and assess the association of risk factors on personality transformation in early childhood.

A considerable body of evidence indicates that there is continuity in childhood personality (for reviews, see Caspi, 1998; Rothbart & Bates, 1998). Continuity has multiple meanings in the longitudinal study of personality (e.g., Block, 1971; Caspi, 1998). *Sameness* (Block, 1971) of personality types refers to the extent to which a person can be characterized with the identical profile of personality traits at two different times. For example, a child who is identified as belonging to the resilient personality type at age 5 and at age 6 can be characterized as high in sameness. We aim to demonstrate in this chapter that there is a degree of sameness in early childhood personality.

The hypothesis of sameness in personality is only reasonable for short periods of time in childhood. This is because traits that may be very salient in early childhood are later eclipsed by traits that reflect the contexts and challenges of adolescence and adulthood. Consider the trait profile defining the undercontrolled personality type. The item "stays close to mom" is very characteristic of children of this type. However, it is unlikely that the same item would be characteristic of any 16-year-old because in the United States teenagers spend relatively little time at home in the company of their parents (Csikszentmihalyi & Larson, 1984). This means that sameness is probably low between early childhood and adolescence.

However, even if sameness is low, a second form of continuity, *heterotypic continuity*, can be high. Heterotypic continuity refers to personality links in nonidentical patterns of behaviors separated by considerable lengths of time (Caspi, 1998). For example, the undercontrolled 5-year-old who fights often with other children may become the young adult who regularly argues angrily with his wife and children. Fighting with peers and arguing with family members are not identical personality traits. Nonetheless, it seems likely that the childhood and adulthood patterns of behavior are connected (perhaps by traits associated with emotion-regulation and the expression of aggression), and consequently it might be argued that there is heterotypic continuity even in the absence of sameness. Although we do not assess heterotypic continuity in this chapter, it will become the focus of our future research as the sample of the C-NLSY ages and the number of adolescent and young adults with personality type scores grows.

How much sameness can be expected in childhood personality type? Asendorpf and van Aken (1999) found low to moderate sameness in personality type over a four-year time span in a sample of 100 German children assessed at ages 6 and 10 years. Sameness was indexed by computing the number of participants who were assigned to the same personality type at ages 6 and 10, which was about 50%. Because participants might be assigned to the same personality type at the two testing times simply as a result of chance, not as a function of personality continuity, Asendorpf and van Aken computed the kappa coefficient which corrects for chance agreement. In their study, the kappa coefficient was .30.

In this study, we predicted that personality types assessed at age 5 or age 6 would have precursors in personality types measured two years previously, and that there would be low to moderate sameness of type over this two-year period. Confirmation of this hypothesis required (a) demonstration that at ages 3 and 4 years personality types can be identified that resemble those found among 5- and 6-year-olds, and (b) that assignment to a type at age 5 or at age 6 is predictable from type assessed at ages 3 and 4.

More interesting than the demonstration of low to moderate stability is the investigation of factors associated with *change*. In the previous three studies, the weight of evidence suggested that in comparison to children of the resilient type, children of the undercontrolled type have more behavior problems and fare poorly in school. Consequently, it is particularly important to understand the processes involved in developmental change from one type to another: What causes a child of the resilient type to become undercontrolled? How can an undercontrolled child become resilient?

In this study, we approached personality change from the perspective of exposure to risk. According to this perspective, risk factors in a child's environment endanger healthy development. Our emphasis on exposure to risk is generally more consistent with a *diathesis-stress model* of personality change than with models that link particular influences to specific kinds of personality change (*specific influence* model). The diathesis-stress model

63

posits that prolonged stress can effect broad, maladaptive changes in personality that are consistent with preexisting personality tendencies. In this model, it matters little whether it is poor parenting, crowded housing, or economic hardship that gives rise to the stress, as it is primarily the amount of stress, not its origin, that produces personality change. In contrast, the specific influence model posits that facets of personality may differ in their receptiveness to specific contextual influences. In the spirit of the specific influence model, it might be hypothesized that the adoption of harsh physical punishment by parents will increase children's propensity for aggression, but otherwise have little effect on personality. There is so little known about personality change (for a review, see Caspi, 1998) that neither model has compelling support. However, the weight of evidence collected to date favors the diathesis-stress model (Steinberg & Avenevoli, 2000).

Risk factors in childhood assessed in this study included poverty, a single-parent family, poor quality of the home environment, and large family size (these risk factors have been assessed in other studies, e.g., Fergusson, Horwood, & Lynskey, 1994; Weitoft, Hjern, Haglund, & Rosén, 2003). The presence of a risk factor in a child's environment does not inevitably lead to developmental failure; indeed, all of the risk factors listed above—except home environment—probably do not directly affect personality. Risk factors are best understood as probabilistic indicators of poorly identified psychological processes that derail development and increase stress (for a discussion, see Rutter, 2000). Poverty, for example, is a risk factor because, as previous research has demonstrated, it predicts to increased stress and poor outcomes in a variety of domains, including health and intellectual development (for a review, see Bradley & Corwyn, 2002). Poverty predicts these outcomes because it is associated with stress, poor healthcare, impaired parenting, residence in neighborhoods with inadequate schools, few opportunities, and so forth.

Race and ethnicity are also related to stress. In the United States, Blacks are at much greater risk for premature death and a variety of illnesses. This difference in risk is partially attributable to differences in factors related to racial differences in socioeconomic status. Because Black Americans are, on average, less affluent than White Americans, they are more likely to have less access to healthcare and to live in neighborhoods and housing that are associated with poor health. The difference in health risks between White and Black Americans also seems attributable to stress that is directly attributable to Black Americans' exposure to racism and discrimination (Williams, 1999). Although we do not include race in our index of exposure to risk, we do consider it as a predictor of change in personality.

Much of the previous research has suggested that it is the number of risk factors in a child's environment, rather than the presence of any particular influence, that best predicts maladaptive outcomes (Rutter, 2000). For example, Sameroff, Seifer, Baldwin, and Baldwin (1993) used cluster analysis to classify risks into types of risks, and then used these types to predict change in intelligence between the age of 4 years and 13 years. They found that the number of risks, but not the types of risk, predicts to change intelligence. This line of investigation led us to focus on the number of risk factors present in a child's life rather than on the contribution of specific risks in the prediction of change in personality type.

The magnitude of association between risks and change in personality type is likely to be low. This is so for two reasons. First, a participant may be assigned to different types at Time 1 (T1) and Time 2 (T2) because genuine change has occurred *or* as a result of measurement error. As a consequence, the relation of risk to genuine change is attenuated by measurement error, greatly reducing the likelihood of observing a strong association. Second, a meta-analysis of the effects of major life transitions (divorce, etc.) on personality in adulthood suggests that small effects are quite common (Roberts, 2001).

To summarize, our hypotheses were:

1. Personality types in 3- and 4-year-olds can be identified that would be similar to the types previously identified among 5- and 6-year-olds.

2. There is sameness in personality type, indicated by assignment to a personality type over a two-year period.

3. Transitions from one personality type at age 3 or 4 to another type two years later are related to risk factors. Specifically,

a. Transition from the resilient type at T1 to the undercontrolled type at T2 is predicted by the presence of a relatively high number of risk factors in the child's environment at T1.

b. Transition from the undercontrolled type at T1 to the resilient type at T2 is predicted by a relatively low number of risk factors at T1.

c. Transition from the resilient type at T1 to the undercontrolled type at T2 is predicted by an *increase* in risk factors from T1 to T2.

METHOD

Participants

Participants from the studies reported in chapters II and III, for whom maternal ratings of personality are available at age 3 or 4, were included in this study.

Measures

Personality.   Mothers described their children using the 20 personality items described in chapter II and listed in Table 1.

Behavior ratings.   The interviewer judged the child's behavior at ages 3 and 4 in the testing situation in terms of six qualities. Following the procedures described in chapter II, factor analyses of these ratings were used to construct two scales, *Shyness* and *Disengagement*. Scores on each scale were standardized with a mean of 100 and a standard deviation of 15.

School readiness.   School readiness was assessed using the Peabody Picture Vocabulary Test (PPVT). The test requires that children identify pictures that correspond to vocabulary words spoken by the interviewer. The test-retest reliability of the PPVT over a two-year period for children in the NLSY is .66 (Baker et al., 1993). The PPVT was administered to 3-year-olds, but not on a regular basis to 4-year-olds. We used the total standardized score in the analyses in this chapter (with a nationally normed mean of 100 and a standard deviation of 15).

Behavior problems.   Mothers reported behavior problems of 4-year-olds using the Behavior Problem Index, previously described in chapter II and listed in Table 2.

Risk factors.   The presence (assigned the value of 1) or absence (coded as 0) of four risk factors was assessed when the children were 3- or 4 years old (T1). The risk factors were: (a) *poverty*, determined by family income and family size (this variable is provided in the NLSY-child data set); this risk factor was present for 25% of the children included in the transition analyses (described below); (b) *father absence*, indicated by the mother's response that the child's biological father did not reside with the family, characterized 31% of the included participants; (c) *large family* (child had three or more biological siblings) was a risk factor for 32% of the participants; (d) a *poor home environment* (more than 1 standard deviation below the national average on the HOME-SF scale) was a risk for 19% of the participants.

A total T1 risk score was calculated by summing the four risk factors, and ranged from 0 to 4 ($M = 1.07$, $SD = 1.14$ for participants included in the transition analyses).

A total T2 risk score was computed using risks measured at T2 ($M = 1.16$, $SD = 1.15$ for participants included in the transition analyses). The correlation of T1 total risk and T2 total risk was r (2008) = .79,

$p < .001$, suggesting that risk—and by implication stress—was stable across a two-year period.

RESULTS

Personality Types in 3- and 4-Year-Olds

Derivation of types. Personality types were derived for 3-year-olds following the process described in chapter II; the same procedure was followed to derive personality types for 4-year-olds. Similarity between types for the 3- and 4-year-olds and those described in chapters II and III was assessed by calculating the correlation of the vector of mean, standardized scores for the 20 personality items for the resilient, overcontrolled, and undercontrolled types with the corresponding vectors for the 5- and 6-year-olds (e.g., the vector for the resilient type for 3-year-olds with the vector for the resilient type for 5-year-olds). All correlations exceeded .97; from this pattern, we concluded that the personality types identified in 3- and 4-year-old children were highly similar to those found in the 5- and 6-year-olds.

Only one participant per family (the oldest child) was included in the analyses in the remainder of this chapter to ensure that assumptions regarding the independence of observations were met in the statistical models.

Validation of types in 3- and 4-year-olds. We examined behavior ratings, school readiness, and behavior problem scores to confirm that the personality types in 3- and 4-year-olds had the same pattern of correlates as did the personality types identified in 5- and 6-year-olds (chapters III and II respectively).

The analyses of the associations of behavior ratings made by the interviewers with the personality types replicated the patterns found for 5- and 6-year-olds. Among the 3-year-olds, children assigned to the overcontrolled type had higher scores on the shyness scale ($M = 103.9$) than did children of the resilient and undercontrolled types ($M = 97.5$, $M = 98.4$, respectively). Multiple regression with dummy codes to represent the three personality types was used to test the reliability of these differences (the dummy code overcontrolled was coded 1 for children of the overcontrolled type and 0 for the other two; the dummy code under-controlled was coded 1 for children of the undercontrolled type and 0 for children of the other two types). Only the dummy variable for the overcontrolled contrast was significant (overcontrolled contrast:

$B = 6.40$, $SE = 1.02$, $\beta = .20$, $p < .01$; undercontrolled contrast: $B = .91$, $SE = 1.20$, $\beta = .02$; $R = .20$, $N = 1070$). Children assigned to the undercontrolled type were higher in disengagement ($M = 102.4$) than were resilient ($M = 98.5$) or overcontrolled ($M = 100.4$) children (undercontrolled contrast: $\beta = 3.87$, $SE = 1.21$, $p < .01$; overcontrolled contrast: $B = 1.88$, $SE = 1.03$, $\beta = .06$, $p > .10$; $R = .10$, $N = 1070$).

The same pattern of associations between personality types and behavior ratings emerged in the analyses of the 4-year-olds. Overcontrolled children were higher in shyness than were resilient or undercontrolled children (means of 103.3, 98.2, and 98.8, respectively; overcontrolled contrast: $B = 5.08$, $SE = .95$, $\beta = .16$, $p < .01$; undercontrolled contrast: $B = .55$, $SE = 1.04$, $\beta = .02$, $p > .05$; $R = .15$, $N = 1306$). Interviewers judged the undercontrolled children to be higher in disengagement than the resilient or overcontrolled children (means of 101.5, 99.3, and 99.8, respectively; undercontrolled contrast: $B = 2.26$, $SE = 1.05$, $\beta = .06$, $p < .05$; overcontrolled contrast: $B = .58$, $SE = .96$, $\beta = .02$, $p > .05$; $R = .15$, $N = 1306$).

School readiness scores were available for the 3-year-olds in the NLSY. Children of the resilient and overcontrolled types had higher school readiness scores than did those of the undercontrolled type (with means of 90.8, 90.9, and 82.7, respectively). Only the dummy variable for the undercontrolled contrast was significant (undercontrolled contrast: $B = -8.27$, $SE = 1.58$, $\beta = -.17$, $p < .01$; overcontrolled contrast: $B = .09$, $SE = 1.33$, $\beta = .00$; $R = .18$, $N = 1021$). This is the same relation between personality type and academic achievement reported in chapters II and III.

Following the procedure described in chapter II, scores on the subscales for antisocial behavior and internalizing/depression from the Behavior Problem Index were used to construct four diagnostic categories: multiproblem, internalizing, externalizing, and psycho-pathology-free. The association of personality type with diagnostic group was significant (χ^2 [1363] $= 41.61$, $p < .01$). The pattern of association was consistent with that reported in chapter II, with 17% of overcontrolled children, but only 13% of the resilient and 15% of the undercontrolled assigned to the internalizing group. Twenty percent of the undercontrolled children were classified in the externalizing group, slightly higher than the rates for the resilient (19%) and undercontrolled (15%) types. Finally, undercontrolled children were more likely to be assigned to the multiproblem group than were children of the resilient and overcontrolled types (31% versus 18% and 18%, respectively). Together, the findings concerning behavior ratings, school readiness, and behavior problem groups suggested that the personality types identified in 3- and 4-year-olds had the same pattern of correlates as did the personality types previously described among 5- and 6-year-olds.

Stability

Table 10 presents the cross-tabulations of personality type at ages 4 and 6 years and of personality type at ages 3 and 5 years. Three patterns are evident. First, there was substantial stability in personality type across a two-year period. The same personality type characterized 55% of the 4-year-olds (kappa = .32, t = 16.46, $p < .001$) and 52% of the 3-year-olds (kappa = .26, t = 13.88, $p < .001$) two years later.

Second, Table 10 suggests that the resilient type was slightly more common among older children (50% of 6-year-olds and 46% of 5-year-olds in this category) than it was among younger children (43% of 3- and 4-year-olds were classified as resilient).

Finally, stability was lowest for the undercontrolled type: Only 36% of the 3- or 4-year-olds assigned to this type were still characterized by the same type two years later.

Transitions

Two types of transitions between personality types were examined. One was the transition from resilient at T1 (when the child was either 3 or 4 years old) to undercontrolled at T2 (when the child was either 5 or 6 years old). Children characterized by this pattern were compared with children who

TABLE 10

STABILITY OF PERSONALITY TYPE OVER A TWO-YEAR PERIOD

| Age 4 | Age 6 Type | | | |
	Resilient	Overcontrolled	Undercontrolled	Total
Age 4 to Age 6				
Resilient	423	105	86	614
Overcontrolled	141	248	59	448
Undercontrolled	146	73	122	341
Total	710	426	267	1403

| Age 3 | Age 5 Type | | | |
	Resilient	Overcontrolled	Undercontrolled	Total
Age 3 to Age 5				
Resilient	407	141	121	669
Overcontrolled	180	287	79	546
Undercontrolled	407	81	116	326
Total	716	509	316	1541

were of the resilient type at both testing times (the former group coded as 1, the latter as 0 in the analysis of this transition type). We also examined the transition from undercontrolled at T1 to resilient at T2 (coded as 1 for the relevant analysis) and compared children showing this pattern with children who were undercontrolled at T1 and T2 (this group coded as 0). The scores for the two transitions for both age cohorts were then correlated with the T1 risk score.

Transition from resilient to undercontrolled. Transition from resilient to undercontrolled was correlated with T1 risk scores for both age cohorts: r (456) = .20, p < .01 for those age 3 at T1 and age 5 at T2, and r (439) = .15, p < .01 for those ages 4 and 6 at the two testing times. These findings demonstrate that there was a weak but reliable relation between risk factors and transition from resilient to undercontrolled. For the two cohorts combined, approximately 15% of resilient children with no risks at T1 were assigned to the undercontrolled type at T2. In comparison, 40% of resilient children with four risks at T1 were classified as undercontrolled at T2.

Transition from undercontrolled to resilient. Risk did not appear to be associated with the transition from undercontrolled to resilient (r [206] = − .10, p > .05, for the transition for the 3- and 5-year-olds; r [247] = − .02, p > .05 for the 4- and 6-year-olds).

Change in risk and change in type. To this point in our analyses of risk and personality change, we have assessed the association of change between T1 and T2 in personality type with risks at T1. Because the T1 risk score was highly correlated with the T2 risk score, the analyses reported above focus on personality change in the context of relatively stable levels of stress.

A complementary analytical strategy is to assess the association between change in risk between T1 and T2 and change in personality type. An increase in the number of risks in a child's life between T1 and T2 should heighten stress, which in turn should result in more transitions from the resilient to the undercontrolled type. Specifically, we hypothesized that children who had few risks in their lives at T1 and T2 would be less likely to change from resilient at T1 to undercontrolled at T2 than would children who had few risks at T1 but relatively many risks at T2.

In the first analysis, participants were assigned to one of two groups. The *low stress group* was composed of participants who were (a) assigned to the resilient type at T1, (b) had a risk score of 0 or 1 at T1, and (c) had a risk score of 0 or 1 at T2. The *increasing stress group* was composed of participants who were (a) assigned to the resilient type at T1, (b) had a risk score of 0 or 1 at T1, and (c) had a risk score increase of at least two by T2. The low stress group had 488 participants and the increasing stress group had 30. The relation of risk group membership and change in personality type was quite strong. Forty percent of those in the increasing stress group, but only 15% of those in the low stress group, changed from the resilient type to the undercontrolled type over the two-year period.

Logistic regression was used to predict transition from resilient to undercontrolled from stress group membership, with simultaneous entry of control variables for race/ethnicity, gender, age, and maternal educational attainment. The results are presented in Table 11. Three implications can be drawn from Table 11. First, participants who were characterized by an increase in stress from T1 to T2 were much more likely to change from the resilient personality type to the undercontrolled type than were participants who were in the low stress group. Second, Black and Hispanic children were more likely than White children to change from resilient to undercontrolled. As discussed in the introduction of this chapter, this finding is consonant with the hypothesis that stress effects change in personality structure. Finally, the probability of change in personality type was inversely related to age, suggesting that the probability of transition from resilient to undercontrolled decreased as children got older.

In a second analysis, instead of risk group we used change in the individual risk factors as predictors of transition from resilient to undercontrolled. This permitted an assessment of whether a specific risk indicator was responsible for change, rather than the aggregate exposure to risk indexed by risk group membership. In this analysis, four change scores were used in a logistic regression analysis: change to

TABLE 11

LOGISTIC REGRESSION PREDICTING CHANGE FROM RESILIENT AT TIME 1 TO UNDER-
CONTROLLED AT TIME 2

Predictor	B	SE	Wald	Exp(B)
Hispanic	.50	.32	2.47	1.64
Black	1.02	.31	11.00*	2.79
Gender (males = 0, females = 1)	.03	.25	.01	1.03
Age, T1	−.04	.02	4.81*	.96
Maternal educational attainment	−.17	.06	6.75*	.85
Stress group (low = 0, increasing = 1)	1.07	.42	6.39*	2.92

Note.—There were 518 participants available for this analysis. Stress group membership is linearly related to family income and HOME-SF score, which is why, in contrast to analyses reported in chapters II–IV, income and HOME-SF are not entered as control variables.
*$p < .05$.

poverty (coded 1 if the family moved below the poverty line between T1 and T2, otherwise 0), change to large family (coded 1 if the number of siblings grew to 3 or more between T1 and T2, otherwise 0), change to poor home environment (coded 1 if the HOME-SF score moved from less than 1 *SD* to more than 1 *SD* below the national mean between T1 and T2, 0 for all others), and change in father status (coded 1 for participants whose fathers were present in the household at T1 but not T2, 0 for everyone else). These scores, along with the control variables in Table 11 (variables for race, gender, age, and maternal educational attainment) were used as predictors in a logistic regression analysis predicting change from resilient at T1 to undercontrolled at T2. The control variables had the same relations to change presented in Table 11; however, none of the four change scores was a significant predictor in the analysis (the results of this analysis are available on request from the authors).

DISCUSSION

To summarize, the analyses in this chapter demonstrate that personality type evidences some stability in early childhood. Key to this conclusion is our finding that the personality types characteristic of the 5- and 6-year-olds are very similar to the personality types found in 3- and 4-year-olds. This means that the personality types described in this *Monograph* were found in 28 subsamples (7 subsamples of four age ranges), which is powerful evidence that the types can be reliably identified in childhood. Moreover, this finding makes possible the assessment of stability from one time to the next.

In two longitudinal samples, we found that the stability of the resilient personality type was highest and the stability of the undercontrolled was lowest over a two-year period. In addition, change in personality type was found to be reliably associated with risk. Children whose families are large and poor, whose fathers are not living with them, and whose home environments are rated one standard deviation below the national norm are twice as likely as children without any of these risk factors to transition from the resilient personality type to the undercontrolled personality type. We also found that an increase in risk between T1 and T2 is associated with an increased probability of transition from resilient to undercontrolled, a finding that lends additional support to the hypothesized connection between stress and change in personality structure.

Finally, we assessed the association of change in specific risks to transition from resilient to undercontrolled. None of the changes, taken individually, is a significant predictor of change in personality type. This set of null findings, combined with our findings that total risk and risk group members are predictors of change in personality type, supports our argument that it is total exposure to risk, not the nature of the risks, that best predicts personality change. In the introduction of this chapter, we suggested that this conclusion is consistent with the diathesis-stress model of personality change rather than with the specific influence model.

Although our findings are generally consistent with the small body of relevant findings (Steinberg & Avenevoli, 2000), it should be noted that there are measurement problems that make it more difficult to generate support for the specific influence model than for the diathesis-stress model. Specifically, the exposure to risk measure benefits from the aggregation of multiple indicators, which reduces error. When each risk indicator is used independently as a predictor, there is no aggregation and consequently there is surely greater error in the assessment of risk. This is particularly problematic for this study, because, as we noted, the measurement of change in personality type also has considerable error. Consequently, the associations of the individual predictors to change in personality are likely attenuated by a considerable amount of measurement error. It is certainly possible that future research with more reliable indicators of change in individual risks and in personality type will demonstrate that some risks are better predictors of transition in personality type than are others. However, our findings do not offer this support, and instead suggest that change from the resilient to the undercontrolled type is best predicted by the extent of exposure to risk, rather than exposure to a specific risk.

The magnitude of the associations of risk, and change in risk, to change in personality type is substantial and relevant for social policy considerations. Forty percent of the children whose lives are characterized by an increase in risks over a two-year period change from resilient to undercontrolled, but only 15% of children who live in low-risk environments evidence the same transition. As the previous chapters have demonstrated, children of the undercontrolled type are at a considerable disadvantage in comparison to resilient children; the former have considerably more behavioral problems (approximately .5 of a standard deviation higher) and learn considerably less in school (by one estimate, explained in chapter IV, they fall a year behind academically). These correlates of the undercontrolled type diminish considerably the life prospects of children; consequently preventing resilient children from becoming undercontrolled children ought to be an important priority.

VI. PERSONALITY TYPE AS A MODERATOR OF THE ASSOCIATION OF HEAD START PARTICIPATION TO DEVELOPMENTAL OUTCOME

A principal axiom of personality theory is that personality influences and shapes experience. Extraverted individuals, for example, might find pleasure in a group, but a shy person in the same context may experience anxiety. Interactions between persons and contexts suggest that personality affects, or *moderates,* the relation between a context and behavior. Our goal in this chapter is to explore the moderating effects of personality type on the relation of contexts to developmental outcomes. A variable that moderates the relation of two others "affects the direction and/or strength of the relation between an independent or predictor variable and a dependent or criterion variable" (Baron & Kenny, 1986, p. 1174). In this chapter, we assess the value of personality types as moderators by examining interactions among personality type, stress, and participation in Head Start, the national preschool intervention. Our hypothesis is that the relation of Head Start participation to developmental outcome varies according to personality type.

The Head Start program was developed in the 1960s as part of the U.S. government's efforts to address the educational and health needs of poor children. In the form it reached after rapid early growth, the Head Start program offers comprehensive services in order to improve the school readiness of children from low-income families. Centers participating in the Head Start Program have considerable latitude in designing the services that will be offered to meet the goal of improving school readiness. Despite the variability that the program allows, centers receiving Head Start funds are guided by national standards (Administration for Children and Families, 2002). All recipients of Head Start funds are required to provide for children's health, nutrition, social/personality development, and school readiness; consequently, children enrolled in Head Start are receiving services in those areas. Most children enrolled in the Head Start Program are 4-years-old (USGAO, 2002).

Because there has been no careful, field-based experimental trial of the Head Start Program, the effectiveness of the program is difficult to judge (USGAO, 1997). However, findings from a number of small experimental and quasi-experimental studies suggest that the program has small but beneficial effects on cognitive and social development (USGAO, 1997). This modest set of findings is buttressed by a much larger research literature on the effects of programs similar to Head Start, which also suggests that interventions can influence cognitive and social development (for reviews, see Ferran, 2000; Halpern, 2000).

In the study presented in this chapter, we assessed the association of Head Start participation to changes in academic achievement and behavior between the ages 3/4 and 5/6, and whether this association was moderated by personality type. Our first hypothesis was that children of the resilient type would benefit most from the academic activities offered by Head Start centers. This hypothesis follows in part from the findings reported in chapter IV suggesting that resilient children, in comparison to under-controlled children, derive greater benefit from school. We expected that resilient children would benefit in much the same way from the learning opportunities available in Head Start. Research by Liaw, Meisels, and Brooks-Gunn (1995) is consistent with our hypothesis. Liaw and colleagues found that a comprehensive intervention targeted for low-birth-weight children produced the largest cognitive gains for those children who were actively engaged by the program's cognitive activities. As we reported in chapters II and III, children of the resilient type are highest in engagement, and consequently they ought to gain most from the academic activities of Head Start.

We also tested the moderating effects of personality on the association of Head Start participation to problem behavior. There is some evidence to support the hypothesis that Head Start participation is associated with reductions in aggression. For example, the Early Head Start Program, which is the extension of the Head Start Program into infancy, is related to the reduction of aggression and problem behavior in children (Administration on Children, Youth, and Families, 2001). Consistent with this finding, preschool interventions targeted at disadvantaged children report reductions in antisocial behavior, although the findings from study to study are not completely consistent (for a review, see Yoshikawa, 1995). However, not all of the research reaches the same conclusion. For example, research on the effects of daycare delivered through centers suggests that higher levels of aggression are related to children's out-of-home care (e.g., NICHD Early Child Care Research Network, 2002).

The mixture of findings concerning the relation of problem behavior to children's enrollment in daycare, preschool, and Early Head Start has many sources. Our hypothesis is that the effects of these programs vary as a consequence of personality type. For example, entry into Head Start for overcontrolled children might be difficult, as they are called upon to interact in new contexts with large numbers of unfamiliar children and nonfamilial adults. For overcontrolled children—shy and anxiety-prone—this is likely to be stressful (Kagan, Kearsley, & Zelazo, 1977 offered a similar hypothesis). In analyses with the NLSY, Belsky and Eggebeen (1991) found that children's shyness interacts with maternal employment in the prediction of behavior problems. The direction of the interaction suggested that full-time maternal employment exacerbates behavioral problems in shy children. One possible explanation for this finding is that mothers employed full time are placing their children in centers for daycare, and that this daycare experience is particularly distressing for shy children and consequently culminates in an increase in behavior problems.

Finally, we tested the moderating effects of *stress* on the associations of Head Start participation, personality type, and developmental outcomes. In the analyses in this chapter and in the previous one, a risk score that is the sum of four family indicators for income, home environment, number of siblings, and father absence indexes stress. There is some research to indicate that the factors constituting the risk score might moderate the effects of Head Start on development. For example, based on analyses of data in the NLSY, Caughy, DiPietro, and Strobino (1994) reported that income moderates the relation of daycare to academic achievement scores. Specifically, daycare is most influential for children from very-low-income households. Caughy et al. suggested that this effect might be a consequence of the relation of income to family environment. Their interpretation was that low-income households have family environments that offer relatively little support for cognitive development, and consequently daycare exposure might be particularly beneficial for children from poor families. Both factors identified by Caughy and colleagues—income and family environment—are included in our risk score.

Research on Early Head Start (Love et al., 2002) also suggests that risk can moderate the effects of an intervention on children. Love et al. studied the impact of Early Head Start on infants and toddlers in a large-scale field experiment with a random assignment of children to control and treatment (Early Head Start enrollment) groups. In one set of analyses, control and treatment participants were divided into groups according to the number of maternal risks. Risk factors were (a) failure to graduate from high school, (b) receipt of public assistance, (c) unemployment with no ongoing job training or education, (d) teenage parenthood, and (e) single parenthood. A participant was judged to be at low risk if her or his mother had two or fewer risks, at moderate risk if the mother had three risks, and at high risk if the mother had four or more risk factors. Differences between risk groups in the influence of Early Head Start were found for the cognitive measures, with fewer effects for social outcomes. Participants in the moderate risk group and in Early Head Start were significantly higher on several indices of school readiness than were those at moderate risk and in the control group. There was little evidence to indicate that enrollment in Early Head Start had any effect on those children whose mothers had two or fewer risks. Finally, the researchers concluded, "children in the highest-risk families, however, appeared to be unfavorably affected by Early Head Start participation" (p. 342), a pattern reflected by lower scores on cognitive measures for program participants than for control children.

In the analyses that follow, we examine the hypotheses that personality type and risk are moderators of the association of Head Start participation with (a) academic achievement, and (b) problem behavior. These hypotheses were tested by assessing the contribution of two- and three-way interactions of personality type, risk score, and Head Start participation to the prediction of academic achievement and problem behavior.

METHOD

Participants

As in the previous four studies, we included only one participant (the oldest) from each family in order to ensure the independence of observations. Participants were drawn from the sample of the 3- and 4-year-olds in Chapter V. Only participants who could be assigned to one of two Head Start groups were included in the analyses that follow. The Head Start questions were added to the NLSY in 1990, so participants who were in the 1986 and 1988 cohorts were not included in the analyses that follow because Head Start participation according to the criteria used here could not be determined. The *No Head Start* participation group was composed of participants who were never enrolled in Head Start. Head Start participation was reported by the mothers when the children were 3 or 4 years old (T1) and again when the children were, respectively, 5 or 6 years old (T2). Thus the mothers of participants in the No Head Start participation group reported at both T1 and T2 that their children were not currently and had not been previously enrolled in the Head Start Program.

The *Head Start* group included those participants who had no Head Start participation at T1 (indicated again by maternal report), but who were either enrolled in Head Start at T2 or, if not currently enrolled at T2, had been enrolled in Head Start for at least one year since T1.

At T1, therefore, none of the participants in this study had been enrolled in Head Start. At T2 one group still had no experience in Head Start and the other group was either enrolled in Head Start or had had at least a year of participation in the program. The No Head Start participation group had 2344 participants (1175 males) and was predominantly White (57%). The Head Start group had 83 participants (46 males) and was largely minority (23% Hispanic, 60% Black).

Measures

Time 1. Participants were assigned to personality types and received risk scores at T1 following the procedures described in chapter V. Risk scores ranged from 0 to 4 ($M = .90$, $SD = 1.05$).

A measure of academic achievement, the Peabody Picture Vocabulary Test (PPVT), was administered to participants at T1. The PPVT is a test of vocabulary, and has proven to be a reliable and valid measure of school readiness and academic achievement. The PPVT is standardized to have a mean of 100 and a standard deviation of 15.

Not all cohorts of 3- and 4-year-old children in the sample were tested with the PPVT. In some testing years all children in the NLSY were tested with the PPVT, and in other years only 3-year-olds and those not previously tested were assessed with the measure. Participants without PPVT scores at T1 were excluded from the analyses of the association of Head Start participation to academic achievement.

Time 2. As discussed in chapters II and III, mothers recorded judgments of their children on the Behavior Problems Index. We used the total score, with a standard deviation of 15 and the mean set to zero.

Finally, academic achievement was measured using three subscales of the Peabody Individual Achievement Test. Following the procedures described in chapters II–IV, scores on the subscales (mathematics, reading comprehension, reading recognition) were averaged to form a single index of academic achievement.

RESULTS

Plan of Analysis

The hypotheses required the testing of the two- and three-way interactions of personality type, risk score, and Head Start status.

The first regression analysis compared the T2 academic achievement scores of undercontrolled children to resilient children and of overcontrolled children to resilient children. The interactions of personality type, Head Start status, and risk scores were also tested. As in the studies reported in chapters II–IV, we used dummy variables to compare undercontrolled children to resilient children and to compare overcontrolled children to resilient children.

In the next regression analysis, we used two contrasts to examine the effects of personality type, risk, and Head Start status on the total behavior problem score. Our studies had found that undercontrolled children at ages 5 and 6 were higher on this measure than were resilient and overcontrolled children, consequently it made sense to compare the undercontrolled children to the other two groups.

In both of these analyses, we tested the two- and three-way interactions involving personality type (using the contrasts outlined above), Head Start status, and risk score. This was necessary because the three-way interactions correspond to our hypotheses.

Academic Achievement

Table 12 presents the results of the regression equations predicting academic achievement at ages 5 and 6. First, it should be noted that there were very few participants (only 57) in the Head Start participation group available for this analysis. The small number of participants is partly the result of some cohorts of children in the NLSY not being tested on the PPVT at ages 3 or 4. Because the estimation of the effects of Head Start relies on a small number of participants, the effects should be interpreted cautiously.

The first-order effects indicate that academic achievement at ages 5 and 6 (T2) was best predicted by academic achievement at ages 3 and 4. Second, risk was inversely associated with achievement at ages 5 and 6. Third, Black children were higher in academic achievement at ages 5 and 6 than were White children. Head Start group participation was not significant, and neither were the contrasts for personality types.

The hypotheses of this study are represented by the interaction terms. None of the two-way interactions testing the moderation of effects of Head Start by personality type or risk was significant. However, there was a statistically significant three-way interaction involving the contrast of undercontrolled children to resilient children, Head Start group, and risk score. This interaction is illustrated in Figure 10. As risk increased, resilient children enrolled in Head Start gained more than did resilient children not enrolled in Head Start. At the highest level of risk, resilient children in Head Start were approximately .5 of a standard deviation higher in academic achievement than were children not enrolled in Head Start. Figure 10 suggests that Head Start enrollment was associated with little net effect on the academic achievement scores of overcontrolled children or undercontrolled children. The slopes in Figure 10 indicate that Head Start

TABLE 12

MULTIPLE REGRESSION EQUATIONS PREDICTING AGE 5/6 ACADEMIC ACHIEVEMENT FROM AGE 3/4 FACTORS

Predictor	Model 1			Model 2			Model 3		
	B	SEB	Beta	B	SEB	Beta	B	SEB	Beta
Gender (0 = male, 1 = female)	1.17	.41	.06*	1.17	.41	.06*	1.20	.41	.06*
Hispanic	-.45	.57	-.02	-.41	.57	-.02	-.36	.57	-.01
Black	.94	.58	.04	.97	.58	.04	.99	.58	.04
Age at age 3/4	-.11	.03	-.07*	-.11	.03	-.07*	-.12	.03	-.07*
Maternal educational attainment	1.28	.11	.26*	1.26	.11	.26*	1.28	.11	.26*
Head Start participation	-.18	1.23	.00	-1.93	2.41	-.03	-6.40	2.95	-.10*
Overcontrolled (1) vs. resilient (0), OC/Res	-.20	.46	-.01	-.16	.47	-.01	-.15	.47	-.01
Undercontrolled (1) vs. resilient (0), UC/Res	-.01	.56	.00	-.14	.57	-.01	-.16	.57	-.01
Risk	-.64	.23	-.06*	-.84	.33	-.08*	-.94	.33	-.09*
PPVT at age 3/4	.18	.01	.34*	.18	.01	.34*	.18	.01	.34*
Overcontrolled/Resilient × Head Start				-1.12	2.87	-.01	3.54	3.73	.04
Undercontrolled/Resilient × Head Start				1.38	3.18	.01	9.97	4.28	.08*
Overcontrolled/Resilient × Risk				.45	.50	.02	.73	.50	.04
Undercontrolled/Resilient × Risk				-.03	.46	.00	.08	.47	.00
Head Start × Risk				1.97	1.06	.05	6.03	1.89	.15*
Overcontrolled/Resilient × Head Start × Risk							-4.31	2.53	-.06
Undercontrolled/Resilient × Head Start × Risk							-8.07	2.71	-.11*
R^2 change		.29			.002			.003	
F change (1939 participants, 57 in Head Start)		77.16*			1.18			4.45*	

Note.—Because family income and HOME-SF score contribute to the risk score, they are not included as control variables as they were in Chapters II–IV.
*$p<.05$.

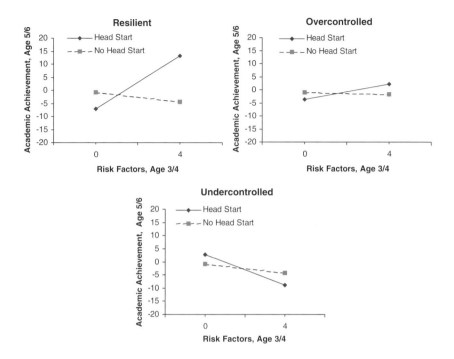

FIGURE 10.—The relation of academic achievement at age 5/6 to risk, Head Start status, and personality type.

enrollment was associated with increasing cognitive gains as risk increased for overcontrolled children. Cognitive gain for undercontrolled children enrolled in Head Start was most apparent for those living in families at low levels of risk.

Behavior Problem Scores

Table 13 presents the results of the multiple regression analyses predicting total behavior problems at age 5/6. The three-way interaction terms added significantly to the prediction of the total score. The nature of the interaction is illustrated in Figure 11. The data presented in Table 13 and Figure 11 lead to three inferences. First, in the absence of Head Start participation, total behavior problems increased with risk at approximately the same rate for children of all three personality types; exposure to risk at age 3/4 was predictive of total behavior problems at age 5/6.

Second, Figure 11 suggests that personality type was a moderator of the association of Head Start participation to behavior problems. Resilient children enrolled in Head Start showed no increase in behavior problems as

TABLE 13

Multiple Regression Equations Predicting Age 5 Behavior Problem Total Problem Score from Age 3 Factors

Predictor	Model 1			Model 2			Model 3		
	B	SEB	Beta	B	SEB	Beta	B	SEB	Beta
Gender (0 = male, 1 = female)	−1.81	.63	−.06*	−1.75	.63	−.06*	−1.73	.63	−.06*
Hispanic	−1.04	.84	−.03	−1.75	.84	−.03	−1.01	.84	−.03
Black	−.27	.85	−.01	−.36	.85	−.01	−.38	.85	−.01
Age at Time 1	.00	.05	.00	.00	.05	.00	.00	.05	.00
Head Start (0 = no Head Start, 1 = Head Start)	.61	1.72	.01	3.10	2.22	.04	3.05	2.22	.04
Undercontrolled (−2/3) vs. Resilient (1/3), Overcontrolled (1/3): UC/R, OC	−3.19	.79	−.09	−2.99	.81	−.08	−2.96	.81	−.08*
Resilient (1/2) vs. Overcontrolled (−1/2): R/OC	−1.12	.71	−.03*	−1.04	.73	−.03*	−1.02	.73	−.03
Risk	1.59	.34	.12*	1.65	.35	.12*	1.68	.35	.12*
Maternal educational attainment	−.90	.15	−.14*	−.89	.15	−.14*	−.88	.15	−.14
Undercontrolled/Resilient, Overcontrolled × Head Start				−6.27	3.93	−.04	−12.50	4.88	−.07*
Resilient/Overcontrolled × Head Start				.87	4.14	.00	5.00	5.15	.03
Undercontrolled/Resilient, Overcontrolled × Risk				.19	.69	.01*	−.12	.70	.00
Resilient/Overcontrolled × Risk				1.43	.71	.04	1.60	.72	.05*
Head Start × Risk				−2.65	1.60	−.05	−1.73	1.67	−.03
Undercontrolled/Resilient, Overcontrolled × Head Start × Risk							8.18	3.43	.07*
Resilient/Overcontrolled × Head Start × Risk							−7.16	4.21	−.05
R^2 change			.057			.004			.003
F change (1959 participants, 73 in Head Start)			14.59*			1.78			3.58*

Note.—Because family income and HOME-SF score contribute to the risk score, they are not included as control variables as they were in Chapters II–IV.
*$p < .05$.

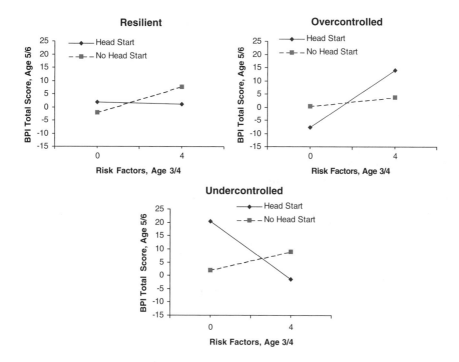

FIGURE 11.—The relation of the total behavior problem score at age 5/6 to risk, by Head Start status and personality type. (BPI = Behavior Problem Index.)

the risk score increased, in contrast to resilient children not enrolled in Head Start. Second, for overcontrolled children enrolled in Head Start, risk was strongly associated with behavior problems. Overcontrolled children enrolled in Head Start at low levels of risk had low scores for behavior problems, but as risk increased, behavior problems increased sharply.

Third, risk was inversely correlated with behavior problem scores for undercontrolled children; at high levels of risk, the undercontrolled children enrolled in Head Start had lower behavior problem scores than did undercontrolled children without Head Start experience.

DISCUSSION

To reiterate, the goal of the study reported in this chapter was to determine whether personality type operates as a moderator, systematically influencing the association between context and developmental outcome. In this study we examined the moderating effects of personality type on the relation of Head Start participation to academic achievement and behavior problems. We hypothesized that personality type was associated with systematic differences in the relation of Head Start participation to academic achievement and problem behaviors. The regression analyses provide considerable support for our hypothesis, showing that the interaction of personality type, Head Start participation, and risk is significant in the prediction of academic achievement and behavior problems.

The analyses of academic achievement suggested that personality type moderates the relation of Head Start participation and risk in the prediction of change in achievement. Our hypothesis was that children of the resilient type would benefit cognitively from Head Start participation. This hypothesis was based on research suggesting that children who appear to be actively engaged by the learning opportunities offered by an intervention benefit most from it (Liaw et al., 1995), and the analyses reported in chapters II and III suggesting that resilient children are highest in this active engagement. Our analyses in this chapter indicate that for resilient children enrolled in Head Start, increasing risk is associated with growth in academic achievement; little change was observed in children between ages 3/4 and 5/6 without Head Start participation. This suggests that resilient children living in families with some level of risk blossom academically in the learning environment offered by Head Start enrollment. There was little evidence that Head Start enrollment and risk are systematically related to cognitive growth for overcontrolled or undercontrolled children.

We also hypothesized that personality type would moderate the association of Head Start participation and risk to behavior problem scores. There is research supporting several of the hypothesized associations. For example, research reviews suggest that Head Start participation is associated with declines in delinquent and problem behavior (e.g., Administration for Children, Youth, and Families, 2001). There is also research suggesting that personality may moderate the association of risk to behavior problems. For example, Belsky and Eggebeen (1991) found that shyness interacts with full-time maternal employment in the prediction of problem scores. Belsky and Eggebeen reported that shy children whose mothers work full time have higher problem scores than do shy children whose mothers do not work. This suggests that considerable experience in out-of-home care—presumably the result for many children whose mothers are employed full-time—is particularly problematic in terms of behavior problems for overcontrolled children. However, to the best of our knowledge, no previous research has examined the interaction among risk, personality, and Head Start participation to behavior problems.

Our findings suggest that the relation of Head Start participation to behavior problems is moderated by both risk and personality type. For resilient children, Head Start participation eliminates the association between increasing risk and increasing behavior problems observed in all children not enrolled in Head Start. It might be concluded, therefore, that Head Start buffers resilient children against increasing stress, at least with respect to behavior problems. The relation of risk to behavior problem scores is moderately strong for overcontrolled children enrolled in Head Start; at low levels of risk, undercontrolled children in Head Start have lower behavior problem scores than do overcontrolled children not in Head Start. Finally, for undercontrolled children with Head Start experience, the association of risk to behavior problems is negative. At high levels of risk, undercontrolled children with Head Start experience have lower levels of problem behaviors than do undercontrolled children without Head Start experience.

Although the results reported in this chapter are consistent with both our hypotheses and previous research, four caveats are in order. First, our emphasis is on personality type as a moderator, not on the effectiveness of Head Start. Our results demonstrate that personality type can operate as a moderator; the relations of Head Start participation and stress to cognitive ability and to behavior problems were found to vary systematically by personality type. Our small sample size of children with Head Start experience precludes any meaningful evaluation of Head Start's effectiveness.

Second, because behavior problem scores were not available for 3-year-olds, it was not possible to control for differences in behavior problems in participants prior to entry into Head Start. An alternative explanation for our findings might be that, rather than reflecting the interaction of Head Start participation with personality, the effects identified for behavior problems reflect preexisting differences between those who will be enrolled in Head Start and those who will not. However, this explanation is weakened by our findings of significant effects for Head Start participation in academic achievement in which it was possible to control for preexisting differences. Third, our findings are correlational. The most powerful evidence for the moderating influence of personality on the effects of Head Start participation is to be found in field experiments with randomized assignment to treatment and control groups, the same kind of research that is advocated for assessing the effectiveness of Head Start (USGAO, 1997).

VII. SUMMARY OF FINDINGS AND GENERAL DISCUSSION

Throughout this *Monograph*, we have argued that a person-centered approach to personality can illuminate childhood development. In this chapter we review the contributions of the research described in the preceding chapters to our understanding of development and identify directions for future investigation.

PERSONALITY IS ORGANIZED WITHIN INDIVIDUALS

Person-centered research aims to place individuals in the explanatory foreground and to highlight the organization of psychological processes within individuals. The person-centered research in this *Monograph* uses personality types to make salient the internal organization of psychological processes of children. Chapters II–IV demonstrate that personality types can be reliably identified in children between the ages of 3 and 6, and that these types are regularly associated with behavior and cognition.

Identification of Types

In chapters II, III, and V, we identified three replicable personality types. The resilient type child is socially cooperative (responsive to adults, collaborative with peers) and gregarious (lack of shyness), and exhibits positive emotions. The overcontrolled type child is extremely shy, compliant, and dependent. Finally, the undercontrolled child is uncooperative with others (noncompliant with adult requests, does not share with peers, fights with other children), and is prone to negative emotions. Each combination of characteristics corresponding to a personality type was found in 28 samples of children (7 samples of 6-year-olds, chapter II; 7 samples of 5-year-olds, chapter III; 7 samples of 3-year-olds and 7 samples of 4-year-olds, chapter V). Clearly, the organization of characteristics constituting each personality type can be regularly identified in maternal ratings of childhood personality.

Moreover, the personality types as described in this *Monograph* resemble closely those that emerge from personality assessments made by teachers (Asendropf & van Aken, 1999), expert judges (Hart et al., 1997; Weir & Gjerde, 2002), and parents (Robins et al., 1996). Nor do the types appear to be an artifact of a particular statistical technique. For example, the types have been identified in analyses using inverse factor analysis (Robins et al.; Weir & Gjerde) and cluster analysis (van Lieshout, Haselager, Riksen-Walraven, & van Aken, 1995), as well as in studies, like those reported in this *Monograph*, that used a hybrid of the two techniques. Finally, the same three types appear in different cultures such as Iceland (Hart et al., 1997), Germany (Asendorpf & van Aken, 1999), and the Netherlands (van Lieshout et al., 1995).

That three childhood personality types are evident in different types of data, collected in different countries and analyzed with different analytical techniques, strongly suggests that the types correspond to genuine organizations of psychological processes.

Coherence of Correlates

Not only are the personality types robust with respect to identification in different cultures, data, and analytic techniques, they show consistent patterns of correlates. We provide quick sketches of these correlates for each personality type. Because the magnitude of associations of personality type to other variables was typically quite modest in our research, the sketches exaggerate to some extent the differences between types. However, the sketches do illustrate the continuity between the core features of the personality types—discussed in the previous section—and the correlates of types identified in this *Monograph*.

Resilient type. Children of the resilient type—cooperative, prone to positive emotions, and gregarious—are advantaged over children of the other two types in terms of problem behavior and academic achievement. The association of type to behavior problems was measured both concurrently and longitudinally in our research. Behavior problems were measured through maternal report when children were 4-, 5-, and 6-years of age (chapters V, III, and II, respectively), and resilient children are found to be consistently low on these measures. Moreover, personality type measured at ages 5 and 6 are predictive of behavior problems assessed at ages 11 and 12, with 5- and 6-year-old resilient children exhibiting relatively few behavior problems at these later ages (chapter

87

IV). Resilient children also receive low ratings on concurrently administered shyness and disengagement scales at ages 3-, 4-, 5-, and 6-years of age. Finally, resilient children are characterized by a consistent academic achievement advantage over children of the other two types at age 3-, 5-, and 6-years-of age (chapters V, III, and II, respectively).

Overcontrolled type. Between the ages of 3 and 6, children of the overcontrolled type—extremely shy, compliant, and dependent—are consistently judged by interviewers to be shyer than children of the other two types. They are also more prone to internalizing behavior problems than are resilient children. There is little difference in academic performance between the overcontrolled children and resilient children between the ages of 3 and 12 (analyses for 3- and 4-year-olds are presented in chapter V; the analyses for 5- and 6-year-olds are in chapters III and II, respectively).

Undercontrolled type. Finally, in contrast to resilient and overcontrolled children, undercontrolled children—uncooperative, prone to negative emotions, and aggressive—are consistently the highest in behavior problems, particularly problems characteristic of externalization. This is true whether behavior problems are measured concurrently with personality type (chapters II, III, V) or six years after the assessment of personality type (chapter IV). Undercontrolled children between the ages of 3 and 6 years of age are judged by the interviewers to be higher in disengagement than children of the other two types. In comparison to resilient and overcontrolled children, undercontrolled children score poorly on tests of academic readiness in early childhood (chapter V), academic achievement at the beginning of formal schooling (chapters II and III), and on tests of academic achievement through the end of elementary school (chapter IV). Moreover, undercontrolled children acquire academic knowledge at a slower rate than do children of the other two types (chapter IV). Finally, undercontrolled children rate themselves lower in academic competence than do resilient and overcontrolled children (chapter IV).

The associations of personality types to behavior problems and academic achievement reported in this *Monograph* and illustrated in these sketches are also consistent with previous research on childhood personality types (this research is reviewed in chapter I). The consistency in both the characterization of personality types and the correlates of personality types demonstrates that the personality typology captures in some measure the organization of psychological processes within individuals.

Specificity of Correlates

One shortcoming of personality types is that they do not provide the analytical specificity that so often is found in variable-centered studies. For example, our portrait of the undercontrolled child includes both poor academic development and heightened aggression. It might be asked, *why* does the undercontrolled child exhibit these characteristics? Are heightened aggression and poor academic development caused by a single trait characteristic of the undercontrolled child? Are heightened aggression and slow academic development the consequence of two different traits? These kinds of questions might lead to the assessment of the relations between particular traits characteristic of the undercontrolled child and the various measures considered in this study, with the hope of arriving at a model that is more detailed than the portraits offered in this *Monograph*. Such a line of investigation is characteristic of personality trait research, as described in chapter I.

When the connection of personality to behavior is examined microscopically, the trait approach is likely to offer the most useful analytic framework. The trait approach allows for very broad personality traits to be split into many narrow traits, and each of these narrow traits can then be tested for an association with a theoretically relevant behavior. Those traits associated with a specific behavior can then be distinguished from those that are not related, a process that leads to the inference that specific trait-behavior links have been identified. This kind of approach is illustrated in complex path diagrams, in which many traits are linked to several different behaviors via complicated paths.

But trait research has its own crucial failing, which is that trait analyses often lose sight of the fact that every personality trait that is put under the analytic microscope is integrated in a system of other traits. When the analytic focus is more macroscopic, when the interest is on the movement of individuals through time, the person-centered approach may be preferable, as this approach capitalizes on the organization of many traits within individuals for prediction. There is certainly a need for future research to compare the advantages of the trait- and person-centered approaches to personality; however, the advantages of each may depend in part on the kinds of questions that are addressed.

Levels of Analysis

The person-centered approach highlights individuals and the organization of processes within individuals. The research described in chapters II–VI demonstrates both that personality types corresponding to organizations within individuals can be identified and that these personality types are useful for understanding developmental trajectories. With the findings of the person-centered research now reported, we return to the issue of levels of analysis. In chapter I we reviewed Overton's (2003) argument that the person-centered approach is one leg of a research triad, to be complemented by the study of intra-individual processes and research on the intertwining of culture and psychological functioning.

Intra-individual biological and psychological processes. An exceptionally important task for future research is to understand the processes occurring within children that culminate in personality types. In our view, biological processes probably are involved in the development and continuity of personality types. There is now a wealth of evidence to indicate that some of the traits that constitute personality types can be linked to biological processes. Negative emotionality and shyness, for example, can be linked to neurological processes (for a review, see Kagan, 1998). Although there is little research on biological processes and personality types, our preliminary findings suggest that there are relations. In a recent study (Hart, Burock, London, Atkins, & Bonilla-Santiago, in preparation), we measured cortisol—a hormone that is associated with the response to environmental stress—in resilient, overcontrolled, and undercontrolled schoolchildren. One measurement occurred during the morning of a typical school day. The other measurement took place in the midst of standardized testing, a period of high stress for students and teachers. The results indicated that overcontrolled and undercontrolled children are reactive to stress, as indicated by substantial increases in cortisol levels between the typical and high stress measurement points. These findings need to be replicated and explored further using longitudinal designs, but they do suggest that there may be biological correlates of personality types. The exploration of connections between biological substrates and personality functioning can contribute to an understanding of the origins of personality types (e.g., Kagan et al., 2002).

Clarifying the connections of intra-individual psychological processes to personality types is also important for future research. Theorists have noted that the processes and characteristics constituting personality can be arrayed along a dimension from abstract to specific (Hair and Graziano, in press; McAdams, 1995; Revelle, 1995). At the abstract end are global personality traits and structures that influence thinking and behavior in many contexts. At the specific end are well-defined patterns of behavior, thought, and emotion that are expressed in particular contexts. Our emphasis in this *Monograph* has been on personality types, which are nearer to the global pole of the dimension than to the specific, context-dependent end. However, our research did examine the association of personality types to a specific, context-dependent personality characteristic: self-perception of academic competence. We found that undercontrolled children perceive themselves to be less competent academically than do resilient children, even when self-perceptions of academic competence are elicited six years after personality type was determined. This finding that personality types are associated with specific, context-dependent patterns of thought and behavior is consistent with previous research on personality types. As we noted in chapter I, research has found an association of personality types to self-esteem, reasoning about friendship, behavior in school (Hart et al., 1997), intelligence (Asendorpf & van Aken, 1999), adolescent drug use (Weir & Gjerde, 2002), and patterns of emotions (Dubas et al., 2002).

What this body of research does not make clear is how these different levels—abstract/global and specific/context-dependent—are bound together. Hair and Graziano (in press) have suggested that the abstract/global features of personality influence and to a certain extent encompass the specific/context-dependent characteristics, which in turn affect behavior and thought. In such a model, the specific/context-dependent elements *mediate* the connection of the abstract/global to behavior and thought. The results presented in chapter IV are only partially supportive of this model, however, as the evidence for mediation of the relation of personality type to academic achievement growth by perceptions of academic competence is fairly weak. Instead, the results of chapter IV suggest that personality types and self-perceptions of academic competence make unique contributions to the prediction of the rate of academic development. This may mean that levels of personality are largely independent, an interpretation consonant with arguments made by McAdams (1995) and Revelle (1995). Indeed, McAdams cautioned against imagining a "hierarchy in personality, wherein smaller units ... are neatly nested within larger units" (p. 379).

One goal for future research is to elucidate the connections of the abstract/global elements of personality to the specific/context-dependent ones. In particular, investigations are needed that examine reciprocal influences between levels of personality. For example, children of the undercontrolled personality type are more aggressive than are resilient children. Moreover, undercontrolled children are more likely than resilient children to interpret the harmful behavior of others as reflecting hostile intent (Hart et al., in preparation). Reciprocal influence could be examined by assessing the effectiveness of interventions designed to change the bias to attribute hostile intent to others (e.g., Hudley & Graham, 1993). For example, if it is more difficult to change the bias toward attributing hostile intent to others in undercontrolled children than it is in resilient children, then it might be argued that personality type exerts some influence on attributional style. It is also possible that by changing the bias toward attributing hostile intent in undercontrolled children their aggressiveness will wane, their social lives improve, and over time their profile of traits will become more like that characteristic of resilient children. Understanding the reciprocal relations among levels of personality must be a priority for future research because a satisfying person-centered account of personality requires a description of the organization of processes within individuals.

Cultural contexts. Throughout the *Monograph* the emphasis has been on the similarity of the personality typology emerging from analyses of children in the United States to the typologies identified in children in other Western countries. There is considerable overlap among these descriptions of profiles of personality traits typically found among children, and this congruence suggests that the typology is replicable in different contexts.

The replication of the typology should not be interpreted as a demonstration of its universality for nothing is known concerning the profiles of personality types typically found in children from non-Western cultures. Certainly future research should examine personality types among non-Western populations of children.

More important, the interpenetration of culture and personality should be addressed in future research. We have argued that the undercontrolled personality type has generally negative correlates: aggression, lower academic achievement, and so forth. It is important that future research examine the reasons for these associations. Certainly it is possible that these negative correlates are a consequence of the interaction of personality with a particular cultural organization, and not the inevitable consequences of personality type. For example, it is possible that undercontrolled children might flourish in cultures in which spontaneity is valued and conformity is relatively unimportant, an environment quite different from that of Western cultures—and particularly schools in Western cultures—in which compliance is valued highly. An account of personality types and their influence on the life course can be greatly enriched by culturally oriented research.

A PERSON-CENTERED APPROACH TO THE LIFE COURSE

Chapters IV–VI examined the value of the personality typology for understanding the life course of children. Runyan (1984) suggested that analysis of the life course requires investigation of behavior-determining processes, person-determining processes, and situation-determining processes. The findings in chapters IV–VI are relevant for each of these processes.

Behavior-Determining Processes

The acquisition of academic knowledge is an exceptionally important activity for children in Western cultures. Academic success in childhood and adolescence improves an individual's chances for satisfactory occupational and emotional adjustment in adulthood. In chapter IV, we demonstrated that personality type is associated with the rate at which academic knowledge is acquired. In two samples, children of the undercontrolled personality type developed academically at a slower rate than did children of the resilient type.

Four comments about this finding are in order. First, the potentially conflating influences of family income, maternal education, and home environment were controlled by including these variables as well as personality type in regression equations predicting the rate of growth in academic achievement. The findings therefore demonstrate that personality type makes its own unique contribution to the prediction of academic growth and decline.

Second, although the analyses suggest that the magnitude of association between personality type and academic growth is small, it is of approximately the same size as the relation of academic growth to family income, or to home environment, or to maternal educational attainment. All of these latter factors are regularly judged to be important in understanding academic achievement. We also estimated that over the course of childhood the achievement gap between undercontrolled children and resilient children grew by about .15 of a standard deviation, a gap that is roughly equivalent to a year of school. In other words, undercontrolled children need seven years of elementary school in order to acquire the knowledge that resilient children learn in six years. We believe that personality type ought to be included along with these factors in every comprehensive discussion of academic achievement because our analyses demonstrate that it is as powerful as each of these variables in predicting change in academic achievement.

Third, our analyses indicate that the association of the undercontrolled personality type to academic decline is not mediated by problem behaviors or self-perceived academic competence. Undercontrolled children do have more externalizing symptoms and these symptoms are negatively correlated with academic development, but these externalizing symptoms (at least as rated by mothers) do not explain the association between personality type and academic decline in childhood. Similarly, undercontrolled children judge themselves to be less competent academically then do resilient or overcontrolled children, but these judgments do not mediate the relation of personality type to the rate of academic development.

Fourth, we found that personality traits constructed from the same items used for the identification of personality types did not predict to the rate of academic development. The trait measures used in this study were limited in several ways. First, the trait measures were constructed from the items included in the NLSY and do not correspond to any of the comprehensive trait models (see Saucier & Goldberg, 2001, for one review of these models). Surely the traits assessed in the NLSY do not span the full range of personality traits, and consequently it is certainly possible that traits not measured in the NLSY might prove to be excellent predictors of the rate of academic achievement. Moreover, the trait measures in this study had modest internal reliabilities, and for that reason the association of traits to rate of academic development might be attenuated by substantial measurement error. Nonetheless, our findings show that personality types identified from the same items used to construct these trait scales are superior for making longitudinal predictions, a finding consistent with the conclusion of Asendorpf and van Aken (1999).

Why are personality types associated with the rate of academic achievement? Three broad classes of explanations deserve exploration in future research. First, personality type and the rate of academic achievement may both be explained by the same process or set of processes. For example, living in extremely poor neighborhoods may lead children to develop undercontrolled personality types and to attend schools that do not provide good educations. Second, personality type may lead children to create academic niches that promote or retard learning. Resilient children, for example, may attend closely to teachers, take good notes, do homework faithfully, choose to sit in the front of the room, and so forth, gradually creating environments for themselves that foster knowledge acquisition. Undercontrolled children may choose to associate with other aggressive children, forget to do their homework, and otherwise create conditions that impede success in the classroom. Third, personality type may elicit differential teaching from parents and teachers. Because resilient and overcontrolled children, who appear attentive to and compliant with adults, are easier to teach than are students who are disruptive, aggressive, and distractible, the resilient and overcontrolled children may elicit better teaching, more support, and higher expectations from their teachers than do undercontrolled children. These three types of explanations are worthy of exploration. As we noted in chapter IV, the association between personality type and rate of academic achievement is significantly large to be of social policy significance, an issue to which we return in a later section.

Person-Determining Processes

There is both stability and change in personality type. Over a two-year period—either from 3- to 5-years of age or from 4- to 6-years-old—roughly 50% of children are characterized by the same personality type at the two testing times. Stability is slightly higher for the older cohort (the 4- and 6-year-olds) than for the younger cohort (3- and 5-year-olds) and for those of the resilient type than for the other two types. Because personality type is measured with some degree of measurement error, these are probably underestimates of the extent of genuine stability.

The study reported in chapter V is the first to assess the correlates of change in personality type, and consequently it is the only existing study to investigate person-determining processes for personality types. Change from the resilient type to the undercontrolled type is associated with a child's exposure to risk. Children developing in an environment with multiple risks—living in impoverished, large, father-absent families with poor home environments—are twice as likely as children with none of these risks to shift from the resilient type to the undercontrolled type, a maladaptive coping response related to declines in academic achievement during childhood. The finding that change in risk status is correlated with change in personality type is particularly important because it suggests that personality type is dynamic and responds to environmental changes. Finally, our findings suggest that it is the extent of exposure to risk, and not the presence of any specific risk, that predicts to change in personality type.

Situation-Determining Processes

Evaluation research of large-scale interventions with infants, toddlers, and children suggests that program participants do not benefit equally (e.g., Love et al., 2002; Liaw et al., 1995; for a review see Ferran, 2000). We suggested in chapter I and earlier in this chapter that children's effective environments may be fashioned by their personality types, and on that basis children of the three personality types may experience Head Start differently. The results in chapter VI are consistent with this interpretation. We found that that personality type interacts with Head Start participation and stress in the prediction of the cognitive and behavioral benefits that children derive from the program. In general, resilient children, particularly those living in families with moderate to high levels of stress, seem to benefit cognitively from Head Start. Resilient children in Head Start are also apparently buffered against the effects of stress on behavior problems. There is little association between Head Start participation and cognitive growth for either overcontrolled or undercontrolled children. However, risk is very predictive of behavior problems for overcontrolled and undercontrolled children enrolled in Head Start. For overcontrolled children in Head Start, as risk increases, so too does problem behavior. For undercontrolled children in Head Start, as risk score increases, problem behavior decreases. Though these patterns are in need of replication, they are consistent with some previous research (Belsky & Eggebeen, 1991; Love et al., 2002) suggesting that intervention and daycare experiences do not have uniform effects for children, with risk and personality both contributing to the variation in the benefits derived from these experiences. Our findings suggest that personality type may moderate the influence of programs like Head Start on children's development.

THE PERSON-CENTERED APPROACH TO PERSONALITY AND PUBLIC POLICY

A person-centered approach to personality can contribute to public discussion and to the formation of social policy in three key ways: effective communication of children's developmental trajectories, the identification of pathways connecting risks and outcomes, and an explanation for differential benefits of participation in interventions.

Research findings are most likely to influence public policy when practical implications are clear (McCartney & Rosenthal, 2000). Because the person-centered approach frames analyses in terms of outcomes for types of children, the relevance of findings is easier to grasp than are the implications of trait research. The research described in chapters II–VI can be readily communicated in terms of types of children and their trajectories over time. Consider the following three statements about the findings from our research:

1. Between the ages of 3 and 6 years children can be assigned to one of three personality types: resilient, overcontrolled, and undercontrolled. Each type has its own profile of personality traits, behavior problems, and cognitive characteristics.

2. A child characterized as undercontrolled at age 5 or at age 6 will, on average, fall behind a resilient child by the equivalent of a year of schooling over the course of elementary school.

3. Forty percent of resilient 3- and 4-year-old children in high risk families will become undercontrolled by ages 5 and 6, a rate more than double the rate characteristic of children living in low risk families.

Findings from trait-based research would be difficult to translate into such readily understood statements. For example, if statement 2 were to be reframed in terms of the traits of compliance and insecure attachment (see chapter IV), it would be necessary to discuss the magnitude of the correlations—the effect sizes—of the two traits to the rate of academic growth and decline. Even psychologists have difficulty grasping the practical implications of commonly reported indices of effect sizes (Rosenthal & Rubin, 1982), and for that reason it is extremely unlikely that those charged with the responsibility of formulating social policy can determine whether the associations to which they refer are of practical importance. To make effect sizes easier for policymakers to grasp, McCartney and Rosenthal (2000) recommended recasting effect sizes into outcomes for different groups of people—in a sense, translating findings into person-centered analyses.

Identification of Pathways

Public policy benefits most from research that explains how institutions, social structures, and economic policies influence the course of child development. For example, Duncan and Brooks-Gunn (2000) reviewed research on the processes that connect poverty to poor child outcomes. They concluded that research suggests six pathways through which poverty produces poor childhood adaptation. Generally, children living in poverty are more likely to have low quality home environments, low quality day care, parents who are financially stressed and suffering from poor mental health, strained parent-child relationships, and homes in distressed neighborhoods (Duncan & Brooks-Gunn, 2000, p. 190). This research is useful for public policy because it improves the design of interventions and informs changes in regulations that are intended to ameliorate the effects of poverty on development.

The findings presented in this *Monograph* trace another pathway between poverty and poor childhood adaptation, and consequently are of relevance for social policy. Briefly, these findings are: (a) undercontrolled children lag behind resilient children in academic achievement, and are approximately a year behind resilient children in achievement by the end of elementary school; and (b) life in environments with many risks apparently can change resilient children into undercontrolled ones, and (c) the risks assessed in this *Monograph* are linked to low family income and residence in high poverty neighborhoods (Lamison-White, 1995). Consequently, the demonstration of a connection between exposure to risk and maladaptive changes in personality type (i.e., the shift from resilient to undercontrolled) has implications for understanding the processes that contribute to the firmly established link between poverty and slowed academic development.

Explanation of Differential Benefits

Program evaluation research aims to determine whether, and to what extent, an intervention is successful in achieving its goals. Typically, the analytic strategy is to test for differences in average scores between those who participated in a program and those in a control or comparison group. If program participants have higher scores for a desirable outcome than do those in the control group, the program is judged to be a success. However, Shonkoff (2000, p. 186) pointed out that this evaluation approach does not address the crucially important question "for whom is it [the program] most effective?" Mean level differences favoring the program group may obscure the important fact that some children do not benefit from, or even may be harmed by, program participation. Shonkoff argued that "those whose needs exceed the capacities of conventional programs [must] be identified, not hidden" (2000, p. 186). This is necessary to ensure that children who do not benefit from program participation receive the support they need to reap the benefits intended by the intervention.

In chapter VI, we suggested that personality types contribute to an understanding of individual differences in the effects of program participation. Our findings suggest that resilient children appear to derive the greatest benefit from Head Start participation. We also found that the association of behavior problems to risk and Head Start participation varies systematically according to personality type. Both findings were aligned in chapter VI with research on other early childhood interventions. Clearly, these findings need to be replicated, and causal inferences will require experimental studies involving random assignment of participants to conditions. Nonetheless, the findings do illustrate the potential value of the person-centered approach to personality outlined in this *Monograph* for answering the question of "Who benefits?" that is so important for the formulation of public policy.

CONCLUSION

That personality types can be regularly identified, are reliably predictive of academic growth, and change as a function of risk—the central findings of the studies presented here—hints at the value that personality theory and research have for understanding children's development. Our hope is that the personality type construct, embedded in a person-centered approach to development, can contribute to a synthesis that both explains how children succeed in life and that provides for effective intervention in the lives of children most in need.

APPENDIX A
CORRELATIONS AMONG VECTORS OF FACTOR SCORES FOR
SEVEN RANDOM SAMPLES OF 6-YEAR-OLDS

		Random Sample 1			Random Sample 2			Random Sample 3			Random Sample 4			Random Sample 5			Random Sample 6			Random Sample 7		
		Factor Score 1	Factor Score 2	Factor Score 3	Factor Score 1	Factor Score 2	Factor Score 3	Factor Score 1	Factor Score 2	Factor Score 3	Factor Score 1	Factor Score 2	Factor Score 3	Factor Score 1	Factor Score 2	Factor Score 3	Factor Score 1	Factor Score 2	Factor Score 3	Factor Score 1	Factor Score 2	Factor Score 3
Random Sample 1	Factor Score 1																						
	Factor Score 2	.00																					
	Factor Score 3	.00	.00																				
Random Sample 2	Factor Score 1	.91	-.07	.26																			
	Factor Score 2	.19	.92	-.19	.00																		
	Factor Score 3	-.11	.18	.85	.00	.00																	
Random Sample 3	Factor Score 1	.30[a]	.87[a]	-.02[a]	.10[a]	.94[a]	.22[a]																
	Factor Score 2	.86[b]	-.08[b]	-.01[b]	.91[b]	.01[b]	-.29[b]	.00															
	Factor Score 3	.09	-.04	.94	.30	-.19	.86	.00[a]	.00[b]														
Random Sample 4	Factor Score 1	.87	-.02	.18	.95	.06	-.11	.11[a]	.92[b]	.20													
	Factor Score 2	.23	.89	-.18	.02	.95	.10	.95[a]	-.01[b]	-.16	.00												
	Factor Score 3	.05	.05	.85	.17	-.07	.89	.13[a]	-.12[b]	.92	.00	.00											
Random Sample 5	Factor Score 1	.94	-.01	.13	.97	.10	-.09	.17[a]	.93[b]	.17	.96	.09	.05										
	Factor Score 2	.11	.94	-.09	-.06	.96	.16	.95[a]	-.10[b]	-.08	-.04	.97	.05	.00									
	Factor Score 3	.00	.00	.89	.16	-.14	.86	.05[a]	-.12[b]	.93	.03	-.08	.93	.00	.00								
Random Sample 6	Factor Score 1	.95	-.03	.06	.96	.10	-.16	.15[a]	.95[b]	.13	.94	.08	.03	.99	-.01	-.02							
	Factor Score 2	.14	.93	-.04	-.02	.94	.20	.96[a]	-.09[b]	-.06	.01	.95	.06	.03	.98	.01	.00						
	Factor Score 3	.03	.00	.92	.20	-.18	.92	.05[a]	-.09[b]	.92	.05	-.07	.91	.06	-.02	.94	.00	.00					
Random Sample 7	Factor Score 1	.93	.12	.00	.92	.24	-.19	.30[a]	.92[b]	.00	.94	.23	-.11	.96	.14	-.12	.94	.19	.33			
	Factor Score 2	-.01	.93	.09	-.13	.91	.35	.91[a]	-.21[b]	.11	-.13	.90	.27	-.09	.95	.18	-.09	.93	-.02	.00		
	Factor Score 3	.15	-.16	.86	.32	-.30	.81	-.07[a]	.04[b]	.93	.15	-.18	.91	.19	-.16	.90	.15	-.15	.79	.00	.00	.00

Notes.

[a] Because Factor Score 1, Random Sample 3, resembles Factor Score 2 for all other samples, it was relabeled Factor Score 2 in subsequent analyses.

[b] Because Factor Score 2, Random Sample 3, resembles Factor Score 1 for all other samples, it was relabeled Factor Score 1 in subsequent analyses.

APPENDIX B
CORRELATIONS AMONG VECTORS OF FACTOR SCORES FOR
SEVEN RANDOM SAMPLES OF 5-YEAR-OLDS

	Random Sample 1			Random Sample 2			Random Sample 3			Random Sample 4			Random Sample 5			Random Sample 6			Random Sample 7		
	Factor Score 1	Factor Score 2	Factor Score 3	Factor Score 1	Factor Score 2	Factor Score 3	Factor Score 1	Factor Score 2	Factor Score 3	Factor Score 1	Factor Score 2	Factor Score 3	Factor Score 1	Factor Score 2	Factor Score 3	Factor Score 1	Factor Score 2	Factor Score 3	Factor Score 1	Factor Score 2	Factor Score 3
Random Sample 1																					
Factor Score 1	.00																				
Factor Score 2		.00																			
Factor Score 3			.00																		
Random Sample 2																					
Factor Score 1	.94	-.08	.13	.00																	
Factor Score 2	.15	.95	-.03		.00																
Factor Score 3	.00	.05	.81			.00															
Random Sample 3																					
Factor Score 1	.98	-.04	.09	.98	.08	.01	.00														
Factor Score 2	.03	.96	.01	-.04	.95	-.06		.00													
Factor Score 3	.02	.13	.75	-.03	.12	.95			.00												
Random Sample 4																					
Factor Score 1	.92	-.14	.26	.98	-.05	.12	.96	-.09	.08	.00											
Factor Score 2	.19	.95	-.17	-.05	.95	-.16	.14	.95	-.06		.00										
Factor Score 3	-.02	.20	.75	-.09	.23	.88	-.03	.12	.91			.00									
Random Sample 5																					
Factor Score 1	.96	-.09	.14	.97	.01	.11	.97	-.09	.10	.97	.06	-.14	.00								
Factor Score 2	.15	.91	.00	.02	.96	-.06	.10	.96	.03	-.03	.94	.16		.00							
Factor Score 3	-.10	.17	.81	-.04	.11	.88	-.06	.08	.86	.05	-.05	.85			.00						
Random Sample 6																					
Factor Score 1	.81	-.09	.19	.90	.01	-.08	.90	.03	-.15	.90	.09	-.14	.83	.11	-.13	.00					
Factor Score 2	.11	.96	-.05	-.02	.97	-.03	.05	.97	.07	-.09	.97	.17	-.03	.97	.06		.00				
Factor Score 3	.36	.09	.50	.30	.10	.75	.32	-.07	.82	.38	-.04	.68	.44	-.06	.70			.00			
Random Sample 7																					
Factor Score 1	.95	-.08	.19	.97	.05	.07	.98	-.02	.05	.97	.08	.04	.95	.07	.01	.91	.00	.33	.00		
Factor Score 2	.11	.96	-.07	.00	.97	-.08	.05	.98	.01	-.06	.98	.08	-.02	.96	.04	.03	.98	-.02		.00	
Factor Score 3	-.05	.15	.77	-.05	.09	.96	-.04	.03	.95	.05	-.07	.91	.06	.00	.92	-.18	.06	.79			.00

REFERENCES

Achenbach, T. M., Howell, C. T., Quay, H. C., & Conners, C. K. (1991). National survey of problems and competencies among four- to sixteen-year-olds: Parents' reports for normative and clinical samples. *Monographs of the Society for Research in Child Development,* **56** (3, Serial No. 225).

Ackerman, B. P., Kogos, J., Youngstrom, E., Schoff, K., & Izard, C. (1999). Family instability and the problem behaviors of children from economically disadvantaged families. *Developmental Psychology,* **35**, 258–268.

Administration for Children and Families. (2002). Head Start Program performance standards. Retrieved June 3, 2002 from http://www2.acf.dhhs.gov/programs/hsb/regs/regs/rg_index.htm.

Administration for Children, Youth, and Families. (2001). Building their futures: How early Head Start Programs are enhancing the lives of infants and toddlers in low-income families. Retrieved June 3, 2002 from http://www.mathematica-mpr.com/PDFs/redirect.asp?strSite=36month.pdf.

Ahadi, S., & Diener, E. (1989). Multiple determinants and effect size. *Journal of Personality and Social Psychology,* **56**, 398–408.

Allport, G. (1937). *Personality: A psychological interpretation*. New York: Holt.

Allport, G., & Odbert, H. S. (1936). Trait names: A psycho-lexical study. *Psychological Monographs,* **47**(211), whole issue.

Asendorpf, J. B. (2000). A person-centered approach to personality and social relationships: Findings from the Berlin relationship study. In L. R. Berman, R. B. Cairns, L. G. Nilsson, & L. Nystedt (Eds.), *Developmental science and the holistic approach*. Mahwah, NJ: Erlbaum.

Asendorpf, J. B., Borkenau, P., Ostendorf, F., & Van Aken, M. A. G. (2001). Carving personality description at its joints: Confirmation of three replicable personality prototypes for both children and adults. *European Journal of Personality,* **15**, 169–198.

Asendorpf, J., & van Aken, M. A. G. (1999). Resilient, overcontrolled, and undercontrolled personality prototypes in childhood: Replicability, predictive power, and the trait-type issue. *Journal of Personality and Social Psychology,* **77**, 815–832.

Baker, P. C., Keck, C. K., Mott, F. L., & Quinlan, S. V. (1993). *NLSY child handbook: A guide to the 1986–1990 National Longitudinal Survey of Youth child data*. Columbus, OH: Center for Human Resource Research, Ohio State University.

Barnett, W. S. (2000). Economics of early childhood intervention. In J. P. Shonkoff & S. J. Meisels (Eds.), *Handbook of early childhood intervention* (2nd ed.). New York: Cambridge University Press.

Baron, R. M., & Kenny, D. A. (1986). The moderator-mediator variable distinction in social psychological research: Conceptual, strategic, and statistical considerations. *Journal of Personality and Social Psychology,* **51**, 1173–1182.

Baydar, N. (1995). Reliability and validity of temperament scales of the NLSY child assessments. *Journal of Applied Developmental Psychology, 16*, 339–370.

Belsky, J., & Eggebeen, D. (1991). Early and extensive maternal employment and young children's socioemotional development: Children of the National Longitudinal Survey of Youth. *Journal of Marriage & the Family, 53*, 1083–1098.

Block, J. (1971). *Lives through time.* Berkeley: Bancroft.

Block, J. (2002). *Personality as an affect-processing system: Toward an integrative theory.* Mahwah, NJ: Erlbaum.

Block, J., & Block, J. H. (1980). *The California Child Q-set.* Palo Alto, CA: Consulting Psychologists Press. (Original work published 1969).

Block, J. H., & Block, J. (1980). The role of ego-control and ego-resiliency in the organization of behavior. In W. A. Collins (Ed.), *The Minnesota Symposia on Child Psychology, Vol. 13.* Hillsdale, NJ: Erlbaum.

Bradley, R. H., & Corwyn, R. F. (2002). Socioeconomic status and child development. *Annual Review of Psychology, 53*, 371–399.

Bureau of Labor Statistics. (1995). *National longitudinal surveys.* Retrieved June 6, 2001 from http://stats.bls.gov/nlsmothr.htm.

Cairns, R. B., & Cairns, B. D. (1994). *Lifelines and risks: Pathways of youth in our time.* New York: Cambridge University Press.

Cairns, R. B., Cairns, B. D., & Neckerman, J. J. (1989). Early school dropout: Configurations and determinants. *Child Development, 60*, 1437–1452.

Campbell, D. T., & Stanley, J. C. (1966). *Experimental and quasi-experimental designs for research.* Chicago: Rand-McNally.

Caspi, A. (1987). Personality in the life course. *Journal of Personality and Social Psychology, 53*, 1203–1213.

Caspi, A. (1998). Personality development across the life-course. In N. Eisenberg (Vol. Ed.), *Handbook of child psychology. Vol. 3: Social, emotional, and personality development.* New York: Wiley.

Caspi, A., & Silva, P. (1995). Temperamental qualities at age 3 predict personality traits in young adulthood: Longitudinal evidence from a birth cohort. *Child Development, 66*, 486–498.

Caughy, M., O., DiPietro, J. A., & Strobino, D. M. (1994). Day-care participation as a protective factor in the cognitive development of low-income children. *Child Development, 65*, 457–471.

Center for Human Resource Research. (1999). *NLSY79 user's guide.* Columbus, OH: Ohio State University Press.

Center for Human Resource Research. (1997). *NLSY/79 1994: Child & young adult data users guide.* Columbus, Ohio: Ohio State University Press.

Costa, P. T., Herbst, J. H., McCrae, R. R., Samuels, J., & Ozer, D. J. (2002). The replicability and utility of three personality types. *European Journal of Personality, 16*, 573–587.

Crane, J. (1998). Building on success. In J. Crane (Ed.), *Social programs that work.* New York: Russell Sage Foundation.

Csikszentmihalyi, M., & Larson, R. (1984). *Being adolescent: Conflict and growth in the teenage years.* New York: Basic Books.

DeNavas-Walt, C., Cleveland, R. W., & Roemer, M. I. (2001). *Money income in the United States: 2000.* Washington, DC: U. S. Census Bureau. Downloaded from http://www.census.gov/prod/2001pubs/p60-213.pdf.

Dubas, J. S., Gerris, J. R. M., Janssens, J. M. A. M., & Vermulst, A. A. (2002). Personality types of adolescents: Concurrent correlates, antecedents, and type X parenting interactions. *Journal of Adolescence, 25*, 79–92.

Duncan, G. J., & Brooks-Gunn, J. (2000). Family poverty, welfare reform, and child development. *Child Development, 71*, 188–196.

Duncan, G. J., Yeung, W. J., Brooks-Gunn, J., & Smith, J. R. (1998). How much does childhood poverty affect the life chances of children? *American Sociological Review, 63*, 406–423.

Elder, G. H. (1998). The life course as developmental theory. *Child Development, 69*, 1–12.

Emery, R. E., Waldron, M., Kitzmann, K. M., & Aaron, J. (1999). Delinquent behavior, future divorce or nonmarital childbearing, and externalizing behavior among offspring: A 14-year prospective study. *Journal of Family Psychology, 13*, 568–579.

Endler, N. S. (2000). The interface between personality and cognition. *European Journal of Personality, 14*, 377–389.

Entwisle, D. R. (1990). Schools and the adolescent. In S. Feldman, & G . R. Ellior (Eds.), *At the threshold: The developing adolescent*. Cambridge, MA: Harvard University Press.

Fergusson, D. M., Horwood, J., & Lynskey, M. (1994). The childhoods of multiple problem adolescents: A 15-year longitudinal study. *Journal of Child Psychology and Psychiatry, 35*, 1123–1140.

Ferran, D. C. (2000). Another decade of intervention for children who are low income or disabled: What do we know now? In J. P. Shonkoff & S. J. Meisels (Eds.), *Handbook of early childhood intervention* (2nd ed.). New York: Cambridge University Press.

Finn, J. D., Pannozzo, G. M., & Voekl, K. E. (1995). Disruptive and inattentive-withdrawn behavior and achievement among fourth graders. *The Elementary School Journal, 95*, 421–434.

Freud, S. (1962). *The ego and the id*. New York: W. W. Norton.

Funder, D. (2001). Personality. *Annual Review of Psychology, 52*, 197–221.

Gottlieb, G. (2002). Developmental-behavioral initiation of evolutionary change. *Psychological Review, 109*, 211–218.

Gottlieb, G., & Halpern, C. T. (2002). A relational view of causality in normal and abnormal development. *Development and Psychopathology, 14*, 421–435.

Hair, E. C., & Graziano, W. G. (in press). Self-esteem, personality, and achievement in high school: A prospective longitudinal study in Texas. *Journal of Personality*.

Halpern, R. (2000). Early childhood intervention for low-income children and families. In J. P. Shonkoff & S. J. Meisels (Eds.), *Handbook of early childhood intervention* (2nd ed.). New York: Cambridge University Press.

Hart, D., Burock, D., London, B., Atkins, R., & Bonilla-Santiago, G. (in preparation). Behavioral, attributional, and physiological mediators of the influence of personality type on academic achievement.

Hart, D., Hofmann, V., Edelstein, W., & Keller, M. (1997). The relation of childhood personality types to adolescent behavior and development: A longitudinal study. *Developmental Psychology, 33*, 195–205.

Harter, S. (1985). *Manual for the self-perception profile for children*. Denver: University of Denver Press.

Holburn, S., Jacobson, J. W., Vietze, P. M., Schwartz, A. A., & Sersen, E. (2000). Quantifying the process and outcomes of person-centered planning. *American Journal of Mental Retardation, 105*, 402–416.

Horn, J. L. (2000). Comments on integrating person-centered and variable-centered research on problems associated with the use of alcohol. *Alcoholism: Clinical and Experimental Research, 24*, 924–930.

Hudley, C., & Graham, S. (1993). An attributional intervention to reduce peer-directed aggression among African American boys. *Child Development, 64*, 124–138.

Hunter, J. E. (2001). The desperate need for replications. *Journal of Consumer Research, 28*, 149–158.

Jencks, C., & Phillips, M. (1998). *The Black-White test score gap*. Washington, DC: The Brookings Institute Press.

Jung, C. G. (1923). *Psychological types*. New York: Pantheon Books.

Kagan, J. (1998). Biology and the child. In N. Eisenberg (Vol. Ed.), *Handbook of child psychology. Vol. 3: Social, emotional, and personality development*. New York: Wiley.

Kagan, J., Kearsley, R. B., & Zelazo, P. R. (1977). The effects of infant day care on psychological development. *Evaluation Quarterly*, **1**, 109–142.

Kagan, J., Snidman, N., McManis, M., Woodward, S., & Hardway, C. (2002). One measure, one meaning: Multiple measures, clearer meaning. *Development and Psychopathology*, **14**, 463–475.

Kohlberg, L. (1984). *The psychology of moral development*. New York: Harper and Row.

Korenman, S., Miller, J. E., & Sjaastad, J. E. (1995). Long-term poverty and child development in the United States: Results from the NLSY. *Children and Youth Services Review*, **17**, 127–155.

Lamison-White, L. (1995). *Poverty areas*. Retrieved June 6, 2001 from http://www.census.gov/socdemo/www/povarea.html.

Laudan, L. (1990). *Science and relativism: Some key controversies in the philosophy of science*. Chicago: University of Chicago Press.

Levine, R. A. (2001). Culture and personality studies, 1918–1960: Myth and reality. *Journal of Personality*, **69**, 803–818.

Lewin, K. (1935). *A dynamic theory of personality: Selected papers of Kurt Lewin*. New York: McGraw-Hill.

Liaw, F., Meisels, S. J., & Brooks-Gunn, J. (1995). The effects of experience of early intervention on low birth weight, premature children: The Infant Health and Development Program. *Early Childhood Research Quarterly*, **10**, 405–431.

Loevinger, J. (1976). *Ego development*. San Francisco: Jossey-Bass.

Lorr, M. (1991). An empirical evaluation of the MBTI typology. *Personality and Individual Differences*, **12**, 1141–1145.

Love, J. M., Kisker, E. E., Ross, C. M., Schochet, P. Z., Brooks-Gunn, J., Paulsell, D., Boller, K., Vogel, C., Fuligni, A. S., & Brady-Smith, C. (2002). *Making a difference in the lives of infants and toddlers and their families: The impact of Early Head Start*. U.S. Department of Health and Human Services. Retrieved June 12, 2002 from http://www.mathematica-mpr.com/PDFs/redirect.asp?strSite=ehsfinalvol1.pdf.

Magnusson, D., & Bergman, L. R. (1990). A pattern approach to the study of pathways from childhood to adulthood. In L. N. Robins & M. Rutter (Eds.), *Straight and devious pathways from childhood to adulthood*. New York: Cambridge University Press.

Marsh, H. W., & Yeung, A. S. (1997). Causal effects of academic self-concept on academic achievement: Structural equation models of longitudinal data. *Journal of Educational Psychology*, **89**, 41–54.

McAdams, D. (1995). What do we know when we know a person? *Journal of Personality*, **63**, 365–396.

McCartney, K., & Rosenthal, R. (2000). Effect size, practical importance, and social policy for children. *Child Development*, **71**, 173–180.

Mosteller, F. (1995). The Tennessee study of class size in the early school grades. *Future of Children*, **5**, 113–127.

Mott, F. L. (1998). *Patterning of child assessment completion rates in the NLSY: 1986–1996*. Columbus, OH: Center for Human Resource Research, Ohio State University Press. Retrieved January 17, 2003 from http://www.chrr.ohio-state.edu/nls-info/nlscya/pdf/attriton.pdf.

Murray, H. (1938). *Explorations in personality*. New York: Oxford University Press.

NICHD Early Child Care Research Network. (2002). Child-care structure → process → outcome: Direct and indirect effects of child-care quality on young children's development. *Psychological Science*, 199–206.

Overton, W. (2003). Development across the life span: Philosophy, concepts, theory. In R. M. Lerner, M. A. Easterbrooks, & J. Mistry (Eds.), *Comprehensive handbook of psychology: Developmental psychology, Vol. 6*. Editor-in-Chief: Irving B. Weiner. New York: Wiley.

Phelps, E., & Damon, W. (1989). Problem solving with equals: Peer collaboration as a context for learning mathematics and spatial concepts. *Journal of Educational Psychology*, **81**, 639–646.

Phillips, M., Crouse, J., & Ralph, J. (1998). Does the Black-White test score gap widen after children enter school? In C. Jencks & M. Phillips (Eds.), *The Black-White test score gap*. Washington, DC: The Brookings Institute Press.

Piaget, J. (1965). *The moral judgment of the child*. New York: Free Press. (Original work published 1932)

Revelle, W. (1995). Personality processes. *Annual Review of Psychology*, **46**, 295–328.

Roberts, B. (2001). A meta-analysis of the effects of major life transitions on personality. Manuscript in preparation.

Robins, R. W., John, O. P., Caspi, A., Moffitt, T. E., & Stouthamer-Loeber, M. (1996). Resilient, overcontrolled, and undercontrolled boys: Three replicable personality types. *Journal of Personality and Social Psychology*, **70**, 157–171.

Rosenthal, R. (1990). Replication in behavioral research. *Journal of Social Behavior and Personality*, **5**, 1–30.

Rosenthal, R., & Rubin, D. B. (1982). A simple, general purpose display of magnitude of experimental effect. *Journal of Educational Psychology*, **74**, 166–169.

Rothbart, M. K., & Bates, J. E. (1998). Temperament. In N. Eisenberg (Vol. Ed.), *Handbook of child psychology. Vol. 3: Social, emotional, and personality development*. New York: Wiley.

Runyan, W. M. (1978). The life course as a theoretical orientation: Sequences of person-situation interaction. *Journal of Personality*, **46**, 569–593.

Runyan, W. M. (1984). *Life histories and psychobiography: Explorations in theory and method*. New York: Oxford University Press.

Rutter, M. (2000). Resilience reconsidered: Conceptual considerations, empirical findings, and policy implications. In J. P. Shonkoff & S. J. Meisels (Eds.), *Handbook of early childhood intervention* (2nd ed.). New York: Cambridge University Press.

Sameroff, A. J., Seifer, R., Baldwin, A., & Baldwin, C. (1993). Stability of intelligence from preschool to adolescence: The influence of social and family risk factors. *Child Development*, **64**, 80–97.

Saucier, G., & Goldberg, L. R. (2001). Lexical studies of indigenous personality factors: Premises, products, and prospects. *Journal of Personality*, **69**, 847–879.

Schimmack, U., Radhakrishnan, P., Oishi, S., Dzokoto, V., & Ahadi, S. (2002). Culture, personality, and subjective well-being: Integrating process models of life satisfaction. *Journal of Personality and Social Psychology*, **82**, 582–593.

Schmidt, F. L. (1992). What do data really mean?: Research findings, meta-analysis, and cumulative knowledge in psychology. *American Psychologist*, **47**, 1173–1181.

Schweinhart, L. J., Barnes, H. V., Weikart, D. P., Barnett, W. S., & Epstein, A. S. (1993). *Significant benefits: The High/Scope Perry Preschool study through age 27*. Ypsilanti, MI: High/Scope Press.

Shonkoff, J. P. (2000). Science, policy, and practice: Three cultures in search of a shared mission. *Child Development*, **71**, 181–187.

Singer, B., Ryff, C. D., Carr, D., & Magee, W. J. (1998). Linking life histories and mental health: A person-centered strategy. *Sociological Methodology*, **28**, 1–51.

Singer, B. H., & Ryff, C. D. (2001). *New horizons in health: An integrative approach*. Washington, DC: National Research Council.

Steinberg, L., & Avenevoli, S. (2000). The role of context in the development of psychopathology: A conceptual framework and some speculative propositions. *Child Development,* **71**, 66–74.

Thompson, B. (2000). Q-technique factor analysis: One variation on the two-mode factor analyis of variables. In L. G. Grimm and P. R. Yarnold (Eds.), *Reading and understanding more multivariate statistics*. Washington, DC: American Psychological Association.

United States General Accounting Office. (2002). Head Start and even start: Greater collaboration needed on measures of adult education and literacy. Unpublished report. Retrieved May 8, 2002 from http://www.gao.gov/new.items/d02348.pdf.

United States General Accounting Office. (1997). Head Start: Research provides little information on impact of current program. Unpublished report. Retrieved May 16, 2002 from http://www2.acf.dhhs.gov/programs/hsb/hsreac/hehs-97-59.pdf.

van Lieshout, C. F. M., Haselager, G. J. T., Riksen-Walraven, J. M., & van Aken, M. A. G. (1995). *Personality development in middle childhood*. In D. Hart (Chair), The contribution of childhood personality to adolescent competence: Insights from longitudinal studies from three societies. Symposium presented at the Biennial Meetings of the Society for Research in Child Development, Indianapolis, Indiana, USA.

Weir, R. C., & Gjerde, P. F. (2002). Preschool personality prototypes: Internal coherence, cross-study replicability, and developmental outcomes in adolescence. *Personality and Social Psychology Bulletin,* **28**, 1229–1241.

Weitoft, G. R., Hjern, A., Haglund, B., Rosén, M. (2003). Mortality, severe morbidity, and injury in children living with single parents in Sweden: A population-based study. *Lancet,* **361**, 289–296.

Willett, J. B. (1988). Questions and answers in the measurement of change. In E. Z. Rothkopf (Ed.), *Review of research in education, Vol. 15*. Washington, DC: American Educational Research Association.

Williams, D. R. (1999). Race, socioeconomic status, and health: The added effects of racism and discrimination. *Annals of the New York Academy of Sciences,* **896**, 173–188.

Winship, C., & Korenman, S. D. (1999). Economic success and the evolution of schooling and mental ability. In S. E. Mayer & P. E. Peterson (Eds.), *Earning & learning: How schools matter*. Washington, D C: Brookings Institution Press.

York, K., & John, O. P. (1992). The four faces of Eve: A typolotical analysis of women's personality at midlife. *Journal of Personality and Social Psychology,* **63**, 494–508.

Yoshikawa, H. (1995). Long-term effects of early childhood programs on social outcomes and delinquency. *The Future of Children,* **5**, 51–75.

Zhao, H., Brooks-Gunn, J., McLanahan, S., Singer, B. (2000). Studying the real child rather than the ideal child: Bringing the person into developmental studies. In L. B. Bergman, R. B. Cairns, L. G. Nilsson, & L. Nystedt (Eds.), *Developmental science and the holistic approach*. Mahwah, NJ: Erlbaum.

ACKNOWLEDGEMENTS

We thank Bill Overton, Rick Robins, Patrick Markey, and two anonymous reviewers for their helpful comments on the manuscript. The generous support of the W.T. Grant Foundation is gratefully acknowledged. Address correspondence to Daniel Hart, Department of Psychology, Rutgers University, Camden, NJ 08102 (hart@camden.rutgers.edu).

COMMENTARY

SETTING AN AGENDA FOR A PERSON-CENTERED APPROACH TO PERSONALITY DEVELOPMENT

Richard W. Robins and Jessica L. Tracy

In their *Monograph*, Hart, Atkins, and Fegley make a broad and important contribution to developmental psychology by bringing a person-centered approach to the forefront of research on personality development. Over the past decade, articles by Asendorpf and van Aken (1999), Gjerde, Hart, Robins, John and Caspi (1998), and others have revitalized the person-centered approach and established the existence of a replicable taxonomy of personality types. This new generation of research has spurred an emerging consensus that the person-centered perspective provides an important and necessary complement to the variable-centered studies that currently dominate the field. In our view, Hart et al.'s *Monograph* represents a timely manifesto for the field of personality development.

Hart et al. describe a series of highly programmatic studies that together tell a coherent and interesting story about the nature, correlates, and consequences of personality types. Using data from the National Longitudinal Study of Youth, Hart et al. identify three personality types and demonstrate that these types are replicable, stable over time, and predict developmentally significant outcomes; they identify developmental factors that predict change in type membership; and they provide insights into how personality type moderates the impact of interventions such as Head Start. The research is methodologically strong, using large and diverse samples, longitudinal and quasi-experimental designs, multiple independent data sources, and growth–curve modeling of developmental trajectories.

The findings provide an empirical foundation for future research on personality types, and have important applied implications, particularly for the design and implementation of interventions. More generally, type-based research may help forge a stronger connection between personality

110

and developmental psychology because developmentalists tend to make the child the focus of their science and often incorporate a type perspective into their research traditions (e.g., infant attachment). Thus, the study of types can be an important nexus for the two disciplines.

This commentary is divided into two sections: In the first we describe the specific features and benefits of the person-centered approach; in the second we identify several unanswered questions and suggest directions for future research.

What Is the Person-Centered Approach and Why Is It Useful?

General Aims and Features of the Approach

In our view, the most important contribution of the *Monograph* is its promotion of a person-centered approach. The authors illustrate the usefulness of this approach by demonstrating how typological methods can be used to understand developmental processes and outcomes. The authors do not explicitly specify the central features and benefits of the approach, so we will do so in this Commentary.

The overarching assumption of the person-centered approach is that personality traits should not be studied in isolation. Instead, personality researchers should focus on the total constellation of traits that define each person, and the way these traits work together as a dynamic, integrated system. A central goal of this approach is to identify groups or subsets of individuals (i.e., "types") who have similar configurations of traits and thus share the same basic personality structure (Block, 1971). More specifically, the approach seeks to identify regions in multivariate space where individuals are densely clustered, implying the existence of homogeneous subgroups. Individuals occupying the same cluster are assumed to have a shared etiology and similar personality dynamics.

Psychologists have described the typological approach as "carving nature at its joints" (Meehl, 1979, p. 566) because it attempts to carve human personality into categories comprised of individuals who share the same basic traits. Although contemporary typological researchers rarely make such lofty claims, they do argue, and demonstrate in their research, that personality typologies can be held to the same evidentiary standards as trait-based taxonomies like the Five-Factor Model. In fact, the typological approach, as it has evolved over the past decade, has several key features that parallel the features of the research that led to the development of the Five-Factor Model. First, contemporary typological researchers use sophisticated multivariate procedures to identify types *empirically*; in contrast, most early personality typologies were based on armchair theoretical speculation. Second, researchers now focus only on types that *replicate* and show some *generalizability* across sex, ethnicity, and culture, with the ultimate goal being to construct a universally applicable personality taxonomy. Third, researchers interpret types by constructing elaborate *nomological networks* based on multiple independent data sources. Fourth, researchers have focused on developing a *hierarchical* taxonomy that classifies people both at a general level of broad types and into more specific, narrower subtypes. Fifth, researchers have begun to explore the *developmental origins* and *sequelae* of the types, as well as the processes that mediate the influence of each type on developmental outcomes. Sixth, researchers provide a deeper *conceptual understanding* of the empirically derived types by drawing on personality and developmental theories.

Although much progress has been made on these issues, many questions remain unanswered. In a subsequent section, we will elaborate on these questions and note important directions for future research.

Benefits of the Approach

Focus on intraindividual structure. Taking a person-centered approach has several benefits for the study of personality development. Perhaps most important, it encourages researchers to think about configurations of traits within individuals, whereas the dimensional approach is silent about the intraindividual structure of personality. Adopting a typological approach compels researchers to focus on personality as a system of traits that work together to produce particular developmental trajectories and outcomes. Although the dimensional approach does not preclude examining the dynamics among different traits, the typological approach emphasizes this aspect of personality functioning.

An analogy may help to highlight this potential benefit. An illness such as the flu can easily be broken down into a set of dimensional symptoms, including temperature, degree of nasal congestion, frequency of coughing, and intensity of headache. However, much would be lost in understanding the illness if researchers focused on the correlates and consequences of each specific symptom in isolation from the others. By conceptualizing the flu as a constellation of symptoms that co-occur within particular individuals, researchers can focus on understanding the subgroup of individuals who have the flu, and ask questions such as: Does their illness have a shared etiology, does it follow the same course over time, and do the same interventions reduce or eliminate the symptoms?

Descriptive efficiency. A second benefit is that taxonomies, such as the three personality types examined by Hart et al., are efficient classification systems. Indeed, this is the power of a taxonomy: By classifying something, we learn a great deal about it because members of the same category share many features, outcomes, and correlates. Although it has been argued that as psychology progresses as a science researchers must move from a typological to dimensional perspective, in the natural sciences "type-like" conceptualizations are both common and useful. In fact, in the natural sciences, taxonomies are typically used to classify the basic subject matter of the discipline (e.g., animals, stars, chemical elements), not the traits or features of the subject matter. For example, the Linnaean taxonomy classifies animals, not the traits that characterize them (e.g., hair, warm vs. cold-blooded). In contrast, personality researchers have focused on classifying traits (e.g., responsible) rather than people. Both are important taxonomic goals, and one should not be neglected in favor of the other.

Current typological approaches to personality, such as the one described in the *Monograph*, are purely descriptive, based on phenotypic similarities and differences. However, as these systems advance, researchers can work toward an explanatory taxonomy of personality types. Such a system might classify people according to their developmental origins (common genetic and environmental roots), thereby providing an overarching framework for *why* different children have different personalities. By delving into the etiology and psychological dynamics of each personality type, we can eventually learn more about the mechanisms that drive behavior and the role of individual differences in personality. A similar progression has occurred in natural science typologies, where descriptive taxonomies have often paved the way for explanatory ones. The Linnaean taxonomy originated as a purely descriptive system, based on phenotypic similarities and differences among species, but it was modified in light of Darwin's theory of natural selection to become an explanatory taxonomy based on phylogenetic similarities and differences.

Types as moderator variables. A third benefit of the approach is that personality typologies can facilitate the search for moderator variables. In developmental research, moderators often take the form of subgroups of individuals who show differential responses to environmental experiences or interventions. The search for such moderators is rarely theory driven and instead tends to be based on demographic variables such as gender, ethnicity, and social class. The availability of a personality typology provides a system for classifying individuals into subgroups defined by psychological characteristics, which are likely to interact with interventions and other environmental effects. Hart et al. found, for example, that personality type moderates the long-term effects of the

Head Start program. To the extent that types are embedded in a nomological network with rich theoretical connections, researchers will have a stronger rationale for generating hypotheses about the circumstances under which subgroup differences might emerge.

Predictive validity. There are several empirical benefits associated with assessing and conceptualizing personality in terms of types. Most notably, as Hart et al. showed, types can have greater predictive validity than traits (but see Costa, Herbst, McCrae, Samuels, & Ozer, 2002). The presence of an interaction between type and an intervention, such as the Head Start program, can also improve prediction by showing that the intervention works better for some children than for others. This kind of interaction has important implications for policymakers (e.g., it may be wise to use Head Start programs only with certain subgroups of children and to design new interventions targeted at the subgroups that benefited the least), and for program evaluators (e.g., a blanket evaluation collapsed across all children would hide the greater benefit to certain children). However, because participants were not randomly assigned to the Head Start program, some of the interaction effects documented in the *Monograph* could reflect selection rather than response or evocation effects; that is, individuals who were enrolled in the Head Start program might differ on some relevant variable from those who were not.

For developmental researchers, adopting a type approach is particularly important because is it unlikely that environmental events and contexts ever influence a single trait in isolation. Parents, teachers, and other socializing agents interact with the whole child, not with one trait at a time. The way a child responds to a complex environment like the Head Start program will depend on the child's unique configuration of traits, not just his or her level on a single dimension like extraversion.

Conceptual clarity and intuitive appeal. The type approach also has practical advantages because lay people generally think of personality in terms of types (e.g., "He's a bully"), not traits. Types are intuitively appealing and, although science should not be constrained to our intuitions, this is not a trivial point when it comes to communicating findings to those who make decisions and allocate resources to intervention programs. Findings concerning types are much easier to communicate to the public than are findings concerning dimensions. For example, Hart et al.'s finding that Resilient children show more adaptive outcomes is easier to explain to clinicians, counselors, educators, parents, and policymakers than is research showing how the Big Five dimensions relate to similar outcomes. In fact, when discussing correlational research on traits with the general public, researchers often describe dimensional findings in type terms, by labeling the extremes of the dimension.

By highlighting the benefits of the person-centered approach, we are not discounting the importance of traditional dimensional approaches. Rather, like Hart et al. and Gordon Allport, we believe that "No doors should be closed in the study of personality" (Allport, 1946; pp. 133–134). Typological and dimensional frameworks can co-exist and fruitfully inform each other, as they do in other areas of psychology. For example, Ainsworth (Ainsworth, Blehar, Waters & Wall, 1978) originally conceived of attachment patterns as discrete types, each with a clear set of consequences and correlates for development and relationships. The classification of a child as "secure" has an intuitive appeal that rings true to parents, and allows for the "I know children like that" sense of recognition that is absent from describing a child as low in Avoidance and low in Anxiety. In fact, regardless of whether one believes that attachment styles reflect discrete taxons (Fraley & Spieker, 2003), the field's emphasis on types rather than dimensions may be one important reason why the theory became so prominent. The emphasis on attachment types, and consequently on the dynamics of particular subgroups of children, prompted researchers to conceptualize attachment-related thoughts, feelings, and behaviors in terms of an underlying, evolved neurobiological attachment system. This kind of thinking can be conceptually richer than defining attachment in terms of a person's scores on isolated dimensions, such as anxiety and avoidance. Consequently, in some contexts attachment researchers find it beneficial to think about and analyze data using a typological approach, whereas in other contexts they find a dimensional approach more useful, as is illustrated by a recent debate in *Developmental Psychology* (Dannemiller, 2003). Thus, researchers might do well by reframing the question from "Which is better—types or traits?" to "Under what circumstances is one more appropriate or predictive than the other?"

In summary, personality typologies facilitate the three basic goals of science: description, prediction, and explanation. We now turn to the many exciting avenues for future research in this area.

Future Directions and Unanswered Questions

Refining the Taxonomy

The search for additional broad types. Research accumulating over the past decade suggests that, at the broadest level, there are three personality types that generally replicate across childhood (Hart et al., this issue), adolescence (Robins, John, Caspi, Moffitt, & Stouthamer-Loeber, 1996), and adulthood (Asendorpf, Borkenau, Ostendorf, & van Aken, 2001). Yet, the question remains: Are there really three and only three broad types? Although some studies have found additional types (e.g., Barbaranelli, 2002; Caspi & Silva, 1995; Pulkkinen, 1996; York & John, 1992), so far none of these has replicated consistently across studies. These failures to replicate could reflect the wide range of factors that influence the particular types that emerge in a given study, including the language and culture of the judges, the age of the participants, the instrument used to assess personality, and the statistical procedure used to derive the types. Nonetheless, future research should explore whether these additional types constitute independent broad types, or subtypes that can be subsumed within the three replicable types.

Universality of the three types. It is important to determine the extent to which the three personality types are cross-culturally universal, because doing so would provide insights into the extent to which the types are cultural artifacts or part of human nature. The most extreme position would be that humans evolved, perhaps through frequency-dependent selection, to develop as one of the three types. Hart et al. and previous researchers have provided some evidence of generalizability across age, gender, ethnicity, and social class. However, virtually all of the existing cross-cultural studies have been conducted in highly industrialized and Western-influenced countries, including the United States, Germany, Iceland, and Italy.

There are several ways in which the types might not generalize across cultures. First, although three types might be found across cultures, there may be subtle (or not so subtle) differences in the content of the types (e.g., Costa et al., 2002; Robins, John, & Caspi, 1998). For example, the Resilient type that Asendorpf and van Aken (1999) found in their German sample was defined by more ego control items than the Resilient type that Robins et al. (1996) found in their U.S. sample. These kinds of differences could reflect either an actual cultural difference in personality or, because the type classifications are based on self- or other-reported personality descriptions, culturally determined differences in lay theories about personality. Thus, researchers need to clarify the precise nature of the three types, and work toward a canonical definition of each type that transcends cultural differences.

Second, cross-cultural studies may reveal additional broad types that replicate only within particular cultures; for example, Barbaranelli (2002) found a "Non-desirable" type in their Italian sample, but this type has not emerged in any other studies. It remains to be seen whether this fourth type is replicable across other Italian samples or is sample specific.

Third, the frequency of the three broad types may vary across cultures; for example, Asendorpf and van Aken (1999) found a greater proportion of Overcontrollers than did Robins et al. (1996). Asendorpf and van Aken attributed the differences they found to sampling rather than cultural (i.e., German vs. American) issues, but further studies are needed to fully address this question. Similarly, there may be cultural differences that interact with other variables, such as gender. For example, in most studies, the Undercontrolling type has a higher proportion of males than females, but Babaranelli (2002) found more female than male Undercontrollers in their Italian sample.

Fourth, types defined by similar personality configurations might exist universally, but show variations in their expression, development, or correlates. For example, Boehm, Asendorpf, and Avia (2002) found that Spanish Resilients were more agreeable than German Resilients, whereas Spanish Overcontrollers were less agreeable than German Overcontrollers.

The search for subtypes. The three personality types provide a fairly rough classification system, similar to the general Linnaean categories of bird, fish, mammal, amphibian, and reptile. Despite its breadth, a classification system at this level can be highly useful because identifying a dog as a mammal rather than a fish entails a great deal of descriptive and explanatory information about this animal (e.g., it has hair or fur and evolved most recently from other mammals). On the other hand, we can still make important distinctions among the mammals: dogs clearly differ in important ways from rhesus monkeys. For this reason, the animal taxonomy, like most other natural science taxonomic systems, is hierarchical and makes many more distinctions than the broad classes. Thus, a complete personality typology should provide a way to classify people into broad types such as those described by Hart et al., and into more specific subtypes that afford a more fine-grained level of description and understanding than the three broad types alone.

Robins et al. (1998) began this task by identifying subtypes in a sample of adolescent boys. There were no replicable subtypes within the relatively small group of Overcontrollers, but there were two in the Resilient group ("Agentic" and "Communal") and two in the Undercontrolling group ("Antisocial" and "Impulsive"). Each subtype had a distinct personality profile and developmental correlates. However, subsequent attempts to identify subtypes have failed to replicate these findings or to find other subtypes that replicate across studies (Boehm et al., 2002; Schnabel, Asendorpf, & Ostendorf, 2002). The difficulty that type researchers have had in uncovering the hierarchical structure of the typology is not surprising given how elusive the goal of fleshing out the facets of the Big Five dimensions has proved to be. Future research is thus needed to determine the subtaxonomic structure of personality, and to further explicate the psychological nature of various subtypes. Eventually, the additional degree of descriptive precision provided by subtypes should improve the ability to predict important developmental outcomes.

Developmental Origins

Hart et al.'s findings clearly indicate that personality type matters. Thus, policymakers, clinicians, teachers, and parents who wish to change the developmental trajectory of certain at-risk children may need to intervene at the source of the problem, at the root causes of each type. The study of types provides a descriptive map of personality variability that may help us refine our search for distinct developmental pathways. Members of a given type are assumed to share a common etiology and to follow a similar developmental path. But what is this etiology, and how can we trace these paths? As Hart et al. point out, "the developmental and personality processes that result in these types remains unknown, and these processes should be the targets of future research" (p. 87).

Can we trace the roots of the types to particular configurations of temperamental characteristics or to specific childhood experiences? With regard to questions about nature and nurture, most behavioral genetic research on personality development has focused on dimensional models, and we know little about the heritability of personality types. Rutter (2002; Rutter, Pickles, Murray, & Eaves, 2001) recently described a rich array of research designs aimed at teasing apart shared and nonshared environmental influences and understanding the interplay between environmental and genetic factors, including adoption studies, twin studies, natural experiments, migration designs, time series analyses, and intervention studies. All of these designs could be used effectively to examine the developmental origins of the types.

The strong conceptual interpretation of types—that they "carve nature at its joints"—suggests that they might prove to be even more heritable than traits. Consistent with this view, much of the genetic variance in personality reflects interactions among genes (i.e., nonadditive effects), an idea referred to as emergenesis (Lykken, McGue, Tellegen, & Bouchard, 1992). As a result, certain phenotypic behavioral traits are an emergent property of a configuration of genes, and therefore configurations of traits, or types, may be even more likely to reflect emergent genetic processes.

Once the general etiology of the types is better understood, researchers will be able to search for specific environmental risk and protective factors that might contribute to the development of one type versus another.

Armed with this knowledge, researchers can design interventions targeted at reducing the likelihood that individuals will develop into one of the two nonresilient personality types.

Developmental Sequelae

Hart et al. have done a great service to the field by documenting a wide range of developmental outcomes. Together with previous research in this area, we now know a considerable amount about the sequelae of each of the three personality types. However, thus far researchers have focused on academic outcomes and antisocial behavior, so we know relatively little about how personality type influences other outcomes such as close relationships (with parents and romantic partners), peer relations, and prosocial behavior.

Moreover, in some cases researchers have yet to comprehensively test whether the consequences of the types are confounded by other differences among the types. Future studies need to tease apart those outcomes that are caused by personality types and those that are correlated with the types due to some third factor. For example, Hart et al. controlled for a wide range of variables (family income, maternal education level, quality of home environment, ethnicity, self-perceived academic competence, behavior problems) when they examined the effect of type on academic achievement.

Once it has been established that a type has a particular consequence, researchers need to identify the processes and mechanisms that mediate this effect. For example, Hart et al. show that resiliency predicts positive achievement outcomes, but it is not clear why this relation exists. Is the link due to Resilients' better study habits, their healthy relationships with parents, peers, and teachers, or their ability to avoid deviant and antisocial behaviors? At a deeper theoretical level, one might postulate that the Resilients' presumed capacity to effectively regulate their impulses—controlling them where appropriate and expressing them when doing so is adaptive—might underlie more proximal mediators such as better study habits.

The search for mediators is particularly important given Hart et al'.s findings that personality type moderates the effects of interventions. As Kraemer, Wilson, Fairburn, and Agras (2002) have argued, the finding of a moderator begs the question of what mediates it. In this case we might ask, why do Resilients respond more favorably to Head Start? To address this issue, studies could measure the behaviors, thoughts, and feelings that occur during treatment for members of each personality type, and seek correlations between these variables and the outcomes of the intervention. Kraemer et al. provide a set of useful guidelines to help researchers seek and differentiate the moderators and mediators that contribute to outcomes of interventions like this one.

Toward a Deeper Theoretical Understanding of the Types

Although Hart et al. report a wide range of developmental findings, they do not propose a unifying theory or conceptual framework that could provide insights into the overall pattern. In fact, most previous research on personality types has been largely atheoretical, documenting a set of correlates rather than testing theoretical models about the way the types might be manifested in different developmental contexts. One potentially fruitful means of theorizing about the types would be to link them to extant theoretical models of personality. We already know a great deal about how the types relate to a descriptive model of personality, the Five-Factor Model, but we know little about how they relate to more process-oriented models, particularly those that emphasize cognitive, emotional, and neurobiological mechanisms.

One obvious connection is with Block and Block's (1980) theory of ego resiliency and ego control. In contrast to descriptive dimensions, resiliency and control reflect an interrelated complex of regulatory processes within the individual. Although several studies have empirically linked the types to resiliency and control, the Blocks' broader theory of ego functioning has not been used to conceptualize the types or derive hypotheses. This theory could be particularly useful because it provides a rich source of information about the motives and regulatory mechanisms that drive personality functioning, and the way resiliency and control work together to shape an individual's behaviors, thoughts, and feelings (Block, 2002).

Like the Blocks' theory, personality models based on biobehavioral systems also move beyond classification of phenotypic behaviors and characteristics. Many of these models assume that there are three basic systems: a reward-sensitivity (or approach) system, a punishment-sensitivity (or avoidance) system, and a constraint system (e.g., Clark & Watson, 1999; Pickering & Gray, 1999). Can we draw theoretical links between the three types and these systems? It is possible that Undercontrollers are marked by low constraint, low punishment-sensitivity, and high reward-sensitivity; Overcontrollers have high constraint combined with high punishment-sensitivity and low reward-sensitivity; and Resilient individuals have some optimal configuration, perhaps marked by moderate constraint, relatively high (but not too high) reward-sensitivity, and relatively low (but not too low) punishment-sensitivity.

The three personality types may also be linked to Ainsworth's three attachment styles (Ainsworth et al., 1978). Resilients seem similar to securely attached children, Overcontrollers to Anxious/resistants, and Undercontrollers to Anxious/avoidants. A future study could empirically assess these possibilities, and thereby connect each type to a well-studied domain with an extensive network of correlates.

More generally, the ultimate goal of typological personality research should be to build an explanatory taxonomy that is rooted in psychological and physiological mechanisms. Hart et al. take one large step toward this goal by providing evidence for a descriptive taxonomic system based on a set of replicable categories. Their *Monograph* should be viewed as a call for continued research on these categories, and as providing the groundwork for exploring the internal generative mechanisms that underlie each of the types. We have outlined an ambitious agenda, but one that has the potential to provide considerable insights in personality development.

References

Ainsworth, M., Blehar, M., Waters, E., & Wall, S. (1978). *Patterns of attachment: A psychological study of the Strange Situation*. Hillsdale, NJ: Erlbaum.

Allport, G. W. (1946). Personalistic psychology as science: Areply. *Psychological Review*, **53**, 132–135.

Asendorpf, J. B., Borkenau, P., Ostendorf, F., & van Aken, M. A. G. (2001). Carving personality description at its joints: Confirmation of three replicable personality prototypes for both children and adults. *European Journal of Personality*, **15**, 189–198.

Asendorpf, J. B., & van Aken, M. A. (1999). Resilient, overcontrolled, and undercontrolled personality prototypes in childhood: Replicability, predictive power, and the trait-type issue. *Journal of Personality and Social Psychology*, **77**, 815–832.

Barbaranelli, C. (2002). Evaluating cluster analysis solutions: An application to the Italian NEO Personality Inventory. *European Journal of Personality*, **16**, 43–55.

Block, J. (1971). *Lives through time*. Berkeley, CA: Bancroft Books.

Block, J. H., & Block, J. (1980). The role of ego-control and ego-resiliency in the organization of behavior. In W. A. Collins (Ed.), *Minnesota Symposium on Child Psychology* (Vol. 13).Hillsdale, NJ: Erlbaum.

Block, J. (2002). *Personality as an affect-processing system: Toward an integrative theory*. Mahwah, NJ: Erlbaum.

Boehm, B., Asendorpf, J. B., & Avia, M. D. (2002). Replicable types and subtypes of personality: Spanish NEO-PI samples. *European Journal of Personality*, **16**, 25–41.

Caspi, A., & Silva, P. A. (1995). Temperamental qualities at age 3 predict personality traits in young adulthood: Longitudinal evidence from a birth cohort. *Child Development*, **66**, 486–498.

Clark, L. A., & Watson, D. (1999). Temperament: A new paradigm for trait psychology. In L. A. Pervin & O. P. John (Eds.), *Handbook of personality: Theory and research*. New York: Guilford.

Costa, P. T., Herbst, J. H., McCrae, R. R., SamuelsJ., & Ozer, D. J. (2002). The replicability and utility of three personality types. *European Journal of Personality*, **16**, 73–87.

Dannemiller, J. L. (2003). Attachment security as categorical vs. dimensional: Exploring the issues. [Special Section]. *Developmental Psychology*, **39**, 387–429.

Fraley, R. C., & Spieker, S. J. (2003). Are infant attachment patterns continuously or categorically distributed?: A taxometric analysis of Strange Situation behavior. *Developmental Psychology*, **39**, 378–404.

Kraemer, H. C., Wilson, G. T., Fairburn, C. G., & Agras, W. S. (2002). Mediators and moderators of treatment effects in randomized clinical trials. *Archives of General Psychiatry*, **59**, 877–884.

Lykken, D. T., McGue, M., Tellegen, A., & Bouchard, T. J. (1992). Emergenesis: Genetic traits that may not run in families. *American Psychologist*, **47**, 1565–1577.

Meehl, P. E. (1979). A funny thing happened to us on the way to the latent entities. *Journal of Personality Assessment*, **43**, 564–581.

Pickering A. D., & Gray, J. A. (1999). The neuroscience of personality. In L. A. Pervin & O. P. John (Eds.), *Handbook of personality: Theory and research.* New York: Guilford.

Pulkkinen, L. (1996). Female and male personality styles: A typological and developmental analysis. *Journal of Personality and Social Psychology*, **70**, 1288–1306.

Robins, R. W., John, O. P., Caspi, A., Moffitt, T. E., & Stouthamer-Loeber, M. (1996). Resilient, overcontrolled, and undercontrolled boys: Three personality types in early adolescence. *Journal of Personality and Social Psychology*, **70**, 157–171.

Robins, R. W., John, O. P., & Caspi, A. (1998). The typological approach to studying personality development. In R. B. Cairns, L. Bergman, & J. Kagan (Eds.), *Method and models for studying the individual.* Beverly Hills, CA: Sage.

Rutter, M., Pickles, A., Murray, R., & Eaves, L. (2001). Testing hypotheses on specific environmental causal effects on behavior. *Psychological Bulletin*, **127**, 291–324.

Rutter, M. (2002). Nature, nurture, and development: From evangelism through science toward policy and practice. *Child Development*, **73**, 1–21.

Schnabel, K., Asendorpf, J. B., & Ostendorf, F. (2002). Replicable types and subtypes of personality: German NEO-PI-R versus NEO-FFI. *European Journal of Personality*, **16**, 7–24.

York, K., & John, O. P. (1992). The four faces of Eve: A typological analysis of women's personality at midlife. *Journal of Personality and Social Psychology*, **63**, 494–508.

CONTRIBUTORS

Daniel Hart (Ed.D., Harvard University, 1982) is professor of psychology at Rutgers University in Camden, New Jersey. His research and applied work focuses on personality and moral development in urban youth. With Robert Atkins, Hart directs a nonprofit organization that fosters youth development (the Camden STARR [Sports Teaching Adolescents Responsibility and Resilience] Program) and the Healthy Futures for Camden Youth initiative, which seeks to increase access to healthcare among urban youth.

Robert Atkins (M.S., Rutgers University, 1999) is a doctoral candidate in the Department of Public Health and an assistant professor in the Department of Nursing at Temple University. His research interests include the intersection of poverty and urban development with healthy development in youth. In collaboration with Daniel Hart he cofounded and runs the Camden STARR Program (Sports Teaching Adolescents Responsibility and Resilience) a nonprofit, youth development program that strives to improve the life chances of youth in Camden, New Jersey.

Suzanne G. Fegley (Ph.D., Temple University, 1997) is the research manager of the Center for Health Achievement, Neighborhood Growth, and Ethnic Studies at the University of Pennsylvania. She is currently exploring healthy youth development in the context of low income, urban minority schools and neighborhoods. Other research interests include identity, self, personality, socio-emotional and social-cognitive development in children and adolescents.

Richard W. Robins (Ph.D., University of California, Berkeley, 1995) is an associate professor of psychology at the University of California, Davis. His research focuses on the nature and development of personality and self-esteem, particularly during adolescence. He is currently an Associate Editor of the Journal of Personality and Social Psychology.

Jessica L. Tracy (BA, 1996, Amherst College) is a doctoral student at the University of California, Davis. Her research focuses on self-esteem development and the personality processes that underlie the experience and expression of self-conscious emotions such as pride and shame.

STATEMENT OF EDITORIAL POLICY

The *Monographs* series is devoted to publishing developmental research that generates authoritative new findings and uses these to foster fresh, better integrated, or more coherent perspectives on major developmental issues, problems, and controversies. The significance of the work in extending developmental theory and contributing definitive empirical information in support of a major conceptual advance is the most critical editorial consideration. Along with advancing knowledge on specialized topics, the series aims to enhance cross-fertilization among developmental disciplines and developmental sub fields. Therefore, clarity of the links between the specific issues under study and questions relating to general developmental processes is important. These links, as well as the manuscript as a whole, must be as clear to the general reader as to the specialist. The selection of manuscripts for editorial consideration, and the shaping of manuscripts through reviews-and-revisions, are processes dedicated to actualizing these ideals as closely as possible.

Typically *Monographs* entail programmatic large-scale investigations; sets of programmatic interlocking studies; or—in some cases—smaller studies with highly definitive and theoretically significant empirical findings. Multi-authored sets of studies that center on the same underlying question can also be appropriate; a critical requirement here is that all studies address common issues, and that the contribution arising from the set as a whole be unique, substantial, and well integrated. The needs of integration preclude having individual chapters identified by individual authors. In general, irrespective of how it may be framed, any work that is judged to significantly extend developmental thinking will be taken under editorial consideration.

To be considered, submissions should meet the editorial goals of *Monographs* and should be no briefer than a minimum of 80 pages (including references and tables). There is an upper limit of 175–200 pages. In exceptional circumstances this upper limit may be modified. (Please submit four copies). Because a *Monograph* is inevitable lengthy and usually

125

substantively complex, it is particularly important that the text be well organized and written in clear, precise, and literate English. Note, however, that authors from non-English speaking countries should not be put off by this stricture. In accordance with the general aims of SRCD, this series is actively interested in promoting international exchange of developmental research. Neither membership in the Society nor affiliation with the academic discipline of psychology are relevant in considering a *Monographs* submission.

The corresponding author for any manuscript must, in the submission letter, warrant that all coauthors are in agreement with the content of the manuscript. The corresponding author also is responsible for informing all coauthors, in a timely manner, of manuscript submission, editorial decisions, reviews received, and any revisions recommended. Before publication, the corresponding author also must warrant in the submission letter that the study has been conducted according to the ethical guidelines of the Society for Research in Child Development.

Potential authors who may be unsure whether the manuscript they are planning would make an appropriate submission are invited to draft an outline of what they propose, and send it to the Editor for assessment. This mechanism, as well as a more detailed description of all editorial policies, evaluation process, and format requirements can be found at the Editorial Office web site (http://astro.temple.edu/-overton/monosrcd.html) or by contacting the Editor, Wills F. Overton, Temple University-Psychology, 1701 North 13th St. – Rm 567, Philadelphia, PA 19122-6085 (e-mail: monosrcd@temple.edu) (telephone: 1-215-204-7360).

Monographs of the Society for Reasearch in Child Development (ISSN 0037-976X), one of three publications of Society of Research in Child Development, is published three times a year by Blackwell Publishing, Inc., with offices at 350 Main Street, Malden, MA 02148, USA, and 9600 Garsington Road, Oxford OX4 2DQ, UK. Call 800-835-6770 or 781-388-8200 (US office) or +44-1865-251866 (UK office) or Fax: 781-388-8232 or +44-1865-381393. e-mail: subscrip@blackwellpublishing.com, on the web www.blackwellpublishing.com/cservices. A subscription to *Monographs of the SRCD* comes with a subscription to *Child Development* (published six times a year in February, April, June, August, October and December).

INFORMATION FOR SUBSCRIBERS   For new orders, renewals, sample copy requests, claims, change of address, and all other subscription correspondence, please contact the Journals Subscription Department at the publisher's Malden Office.

INSTITUTIONAL PREMIUM RATES* FOR MONOGRAPHS OF THE SRCD /CHILD DEVELOPMENT 2003   The Americas $375, Rest of World £268. Customers in Canada should add 7% CST to The Americas price or provide evidence of entitlement to exemption. Customers in the UK and EU should add VAT at 5% or provide a VAT registration number or evidence of entitlement to exemption.

*Includes print plus premium online access to the current and all available backfiles. Print and online-only rates are also available. For more information about Blackwell Publishing journals, including online access information, terms and conditions, and other pricing options, please visit www.blackwellpublishing.com or contact our customer service department, tel: 1 800 835-6770 or +1 781 388-8206 (US office); +44 (0)1865 251866 (UK office).

INSTITUTIONAL SUBSCRIPTION RATES FOR MONOGRAPHS OF THE SRCD/ CHILD DEVELOPMENT/CHILD DEVELOPMENT ABSTRACTS AND BIBLIOGRA-PHY 2002   The Americas $369, Rest of World £246. All orders must be paid by credit card, business check, or money order. Checks and money orders should be made payable to Blackwell Publishers. Canadian residents please add 7% GST. V.

BACK ISSUES   Back issues are available from the publisher's Malden office.

MICROFORM   The journal is available on microfilm. For microfilm service, address inquiries to ProQuest Information and Learning, 300 North Zeeb Road, Ann Arbor, MI 48106-1346, USA. Bell and Howell Serials Customer Service Department: 1-800-521-0600 × 2873.

ADVERTISING   For information and rates, please visit the journal's website at www.blackwellpublishing.com/journals/MONO email: blackwellads@aidcvt.com, or contact Matt Neckers, Blackwell Advertising Representative, 50 Winter Sport Lane, PO Box 80, Williston, VT 05495. Phone: 800-866-1684 or Fax: 802-864-7749.

POSTMASTER   Periodicals class postage paid at Boston, MA, and additional offices. Send address changes to Blackwell Publishing, 350 Main Street, Malden, MA 02148, USA.

 **Blackwell E-mail Alerts**   Keep up with new publications from Blackwell Publishing. Join our free e-mail alerting service, and we'll send you journal tables of contents (with links to abstracts) and news of our latest books in your field. Signing up is easy. Simply visit www.blackwellpu-blishing.com/ealerts. Choose which discipline interests you, and we'll send you a message every other week. OR select exactly which books and journals you'd like to hear about, and when you'd like to receive your messages.